HOLD THE SALT!

maureen tilley

Formac Publishing Company Limited

This book is dedicated to my mother for teaching me my way around the kitchen and for all of her help in writing this cookbook.

Formac Publishing Company Limited recognizes the support of the Province of Nova Scotia through the Department of Tourism, Culture and Heritage. We acknowledge the financial support of the Government of Canada through the Book Publishing Industry Development Program (BPIDP) for our publishing activities.

NOVA SCOTIA
Tourism, Culture and Heritage

National Library of Canada Cataloguing in Publication

Tilley, Maureen
          Hold the salt! : 50+ quick & easy recipes to help you eliminate salt from your diet! / Maureen Tilley.

Includes bibliographical references and index.
ISBN 978-0-88780-867-8

          1. Salt-free diet--Recipes. 2. Hypertension--Diet therapy--Recipes.
3. Quick and easy cookery. I. Title.

RM237.8.T54 2009   641.5'6323   C2009-903998-2

Formac Publishing Company Limited
5502 Atlantic Street
Halifax, Nova Scotia
B3H 1G4
www.formac.ca

Printed and bound in China

CONTENTS

INTRODUCTION

Everyone can appreciate a home-cooked meal but at the end of the day who has time to spend slaving over the stove? With today's fast-paced lifestyle, home-cooked meals have definitely taken the back burner. People are reaching for quick and convenient foods and meals to eat on the go. These meals may fit our lifestyle but they are usually not the best fit for our health or our bank accounts. Many of these prepared entrées and meals from restaurants are high in sodium, fat and cholesterol, and low in nutrients. Over time this can lead directly or indirectly to a number of health problems such as weight gain, diabetes, heart disease and high blood pressure.

So who's to say we can't take care of our health, save money and enjoy home-cooked meals all at the same time? The focus of this cookbook is to provide recipes that are blood pressure friendly, quick to prepare and, of course, delicious! It is specifically designed for individuals who have, or are at risk for, high blood pressure, but can be followed by anyone who wants to enjoy a healthy diet.

What exactly is high blood pressure?

High blood pressure, also known as hypertension, affects 20% of Canadians. It is a leading cause of heart disease and the number one risk factor for stroke. As if that isn't scary enough, it is known as "the silent killer" because it often doesn't present any symptoms, explaining why an estimated 43% of people who have it are unaware of it. Hypertension occurs when there is stress put on the blood vessels, causing scarring and plaque buildup which impacts the passage of blood to the heart, brain and other parts of the body. If this disease is left untreated, it can result in weakening of the heart and can lead to blood vessels bursting in the brain, resulting in a stroke. In addition, hypertension can also lead to a number of diseases that affect the tissues and organs, including congestive heart failure, end-stage kidney disease and peripheral vascular disease (decreased blood flow to the legs and feet).

Blood pressure level is measured by systolic and diastolic pressure. Systolic measures the pressure on your heart as it beats, when blood is being pushed out of the heart into the body. Diastolic measures the pressure on the heart between beats, when blood is flowing into the heart. High blood pressure is generally defined as a systolic blood pressure (SBP) of 140 mmHg or higher, and/or a diastolic pressure (DBP) of 90 mmHg or higher.

So you have concerns with high blood pressure … what can you do about it?

Lots! There are many prescription medications that are effective in lowering blood pressure, but lifestyle changes — healthy eating in conjunction with regular physical activity — have been proven to be equally effective to improve your overall health, including the function of your heart and blood pressure levels. Research shows that a healthy lifestyle can decrease or eliminate the use of blood pressure medications; you could even avoid taking them to begin with. It's important to always talk to your doctor prior to making any changes to your diet or medication.

The DASH diet — is it effective? Prove it!

The DASH diet, which stands for Dietary Approaches to Stop Hypertension, is a research-based approach to lower blood pressure. The Canadian Heart & Stroke Foundation and the American Heart Association both endorse this diet. In the healthcare world, particularly among dietitians, it is a diet that is highly supported and recommended. The diet is based on two studies, the DASH Study and the DASH Sodium Study, both of which looked at the effect of diet on blood pressure. In the DASH Study, participants followed one of three diet regimes for an eight-week period:

Group A: typical North American diet

Group B: North American diet with extra fruits and vegetables

Group C: DASH diet with emphasis on fruits and vegetables, whole grains, low-fat dairy products and minimized intake of sweets and red meat.

The results were compelling. Participants from groups B and C showed a decrease in blood pressure and cholesterol compared to group A. Group C (DASH diet) showed the most significant improvement in blood pressure. Within 2 weeks the diet had an effect similar to taking blood pressure medication.

The DASH Sodium Study took a similar diet approach but looked at the effect of sodium (salt) on blood pressure as well. The participants were divided into three diet groups:

Group A: typical North American diet with an average sodium intake of 3300 mg/day

Group B: North American diet with extra fruits and vegetables, and moderately restricted sodium intake of 2400 mg/day (~1 tsp)

Group C: DASH diet with emphasis on fruits and vegetables, whole grains, low-fat dairy products, minimized intake of sweets and red meat and a restricted sodium intake of 1500 mg/day (~⅔ tsp).

As expected, the results showed the negative effect sodium has on blood pressure. Groups B and C resulted in the most improvement in blood pressure — even better results than the original DASH Study. This provided further evidence to support the DASH diet with a sodium restriction.

Key points of the DASH diet:

• Watch your sodium (salt) intake. It's important not to exceed a daily sodium intake of 2300 mg (1 tsp); ideally aim for 1500 mg a day. Keep in mind that most of the salt in your diet does not come from what you add at the table or while cooking, but from prepared foods, processed meats, condiments, sauces, snack foods, canned foods and restaurant foods.

• Increase your potassium intake. Potassium is a mineral that plays an important role in blood pressure control by helping to keep the water in our bodies balanced, including in our blood vessels. The daily recommendation for those with hypertension is 4700 mg. Many fruits and vegetables, dairy products, nuts and legumes are rich in potassium. Some good sources include bananas, potatoes, spinach, tomatoes, oranges, mushrooms, milk, lentils and almonds. Although you can take potassium in supplement form, it is not proven to be as effective as that obtained from food.

• Eat a diet rich in antioxidants. Antioxidants are substances that eliminate and repair cell damage done to our body by harmful chemicals called free radicals. Research shows that damage caused by free radicals may play a detrimental role in the progression of certain diseases such as cancer, hypertension and heart disease. Fruits and vegetables are rich sources of antioxidants, with the colour being an indication of antioxidant level — the darker and richer the colour, the higher the antioxidant content. There's another reason to ensure you are eating plenty of fruits and vegetables.

Improving your lifestyle is all about making realistic and sustainable changes that work for you. Do not try incorporating all of the DASH recommendations at once; it can be overwhelming and difficult to maintain in the long run. The trick is setting yourself up for success. Start by incorporating one or two extra servings of fruit and vegetables throughout your day and steadily increase it to the recommended daily intake. Gradually cut back on your salt intake to allow your taste buds to adjust. Decrease the use of high-fat foods and condiments (butter, margarine, milk and milk products) by lowering your portion size and/or switching to low-fat and fat-free items. Slowly cut back your meat portions by a third at each meal and aim to incorporate more vegetables. Be vegetarian one day a week and enjoy more beans, lentils, nuts and other vegetarian ingredients.

Become label-reading savvy and be aware of what's in your foods. Prepare more meals at home; you don't need a lot of time, just a little organization. This is the best way to control what goes into your food and what you eat.

Controlling hypertension is essential to preventing and/or treating possible side effects of the disease, including heart disease and stroke. Although there is no cure for hypertension, it can be prevented and symptoms can be managed through dietary and lifestyle changes. As mentioned previously, it's nearly impossible to find convenience foods that do not have a negative impact on our blood pressure and heart health. This book is designed to help you overcome this obstacle with quick-to-prepare recipes that are suitable for your fast-paced lifestyle and that, most importantly, contribute to your good health. So, cheers to good food and improved health! Enjoy!

The Nitty Gritty on the DASH Diet

The main focus of the DASH diet is a diet rich in fruits, vegetables, nuts, legumes, fish, whole grains and low-fat dairy products, while decreasing consumption of red meat, butter, high-fat foods and salt. The DASH diet is very similar to Canada's Food Guide but with more specific serving sizes and a recommendation for more servings of fruits and vegetables.

Ackowledgements

I would like to thank the authors from whose books I selected recipes: Elaine Elliot, Virginia Lee, James MacDougall, Brenda Matthews, Linda Bramble and Joy Crosby.

The selected recipes have been modified to meet the requirements of the DASH diet and tested to ensure that flavours are excellent

Food Group	DASH	Canada's Food Guide
Grains and grain products	6 to 8	6 to 8
Vegetables	4 to 5	7 to 10
Fruits	4 to 5	included with vegetables
Low-fat dairy products	2 to 3	2 to 3
Meat and alternatives	6 or less	2 to 3 (2.5 oz, 75 mg servings)
Fats	2 to 3	2 to 3 (1 tbsp, 15 mL)
Nuts, seeds and legumes	4 to 5 per week	Included with meats
Sweets	5 per week	Not specified

These values are based on a 2000 to 2100 calorie-a-day diet for an adult.

The clock beside each recipe title shows you the time you will need to prepare and cook that dish. The first time shown is your preparation time, and this includes any time you'll need to spend cooking the dish (say, frying or grilling). Since this is a collection of quick and easy recipes, you'll find every dish requires 20 minutes or less of your time.

If there is a second time shown, that's the time the dish needs to cook in the oven after you've prepared it. Put the two together, and you'll know how long it will be from start to finish!

SALADS

curried lentil salad, p.20

warm scallop and portobello salad, p.19

YOU DON'T NEED SALT TO MAKE SALADS ENJOYABLE!

Salads are a great way to add to the vegetables you eat. They can be enjoyed as part of a meal or as the main course. You can make most salads more filling by adding lean chicken, seafood, beans or lentils. Be conscious of what you add to your salad; calories can quickly add up if you add too much dressing and/or too much of other ingredients such as bacon, cheese, nuts or seeds.

There is a wide selection of unique and delicious salads to choose from for any occasion. If you're looking for a fresh summer salad I would recommend the Insalata Verde or the Cranberry and Sunflower Seed Broccoli Salad. If you prefer a sweeter salad with fresh fruit, try the Winter Apple Salad with Shallots and Molasses Vinaigrette or Exotic Spinach Salad with a Sweet Poppy Seed Dressing.

black bean and couscous salad, p.21

winter apple salad with shallot and molasses vinaigrette

Joy Bistro, Toronto, ON

The original recipe calls for roasted shallots but this takes too much time to prepare, so to compensate I sautéed the shallots with the apples. It also calls for mixed salad greens but I enjoy the apple served warm, and spinach stands up much better to the heat; besides, it's a better source of potassium. I was able to cut back on the fat and sugar and still come out with an absolutely delicious and flavourful salad.

Salad

½ lb (225 g) spinach
¼ cup (60 mL) goat cheese
¼ cup (60 mL) red grapes, halved
¼ cup (60 mL) green grapes, halved

Shallot and molasses vinaigrette

1 shallot, sliced
2 small cloves garlic
1 tsp (5 mL) fresh thyme
1 tbsp (15 mL) molasses (preferably reduced-sugar)
1 tsp (5 mL) grainy mustard
⅓ cup (75 mL) red wine vinegar
1 ½ tbsp (22 mL) canola oil or grape seed oil
pepper to taste

Molasses apples

2 medium-sized apples, cored and sliced (about 16 per apple)
1 shallot, chopped
2 tbsp (30 mL) molasses (preferably reduced-sugar)

For the salad: In a large bowl, combine spinach, cheese, grapes and molasses apples. Toss salad with vinaigrette.

Serves 4

For the vinaigrette: Combine shallots, garlic, thyme, molasses, mustard and vinegar in a blender or food processor; blend until smooth. While the motor is still running, slowly pour in the oil. Season with pepper.

Makes ½ cup (125 mL)

For the molasses apples: On medium heat in a non-stick skillet, sauté apple slices and shallot for about 2 minutes. Add molasses and turn apples to coat. Continue cooking for another 2 minutes.

Nutrient Analysis per serving:	
Calories: 192	Fibre: 4 g
Carbohydrates: 28 g	Cholesterol: 5 g
Total fat: 8 g	Protein: 4 g
Potassium: 652 mg	Sodium: 112 mg
Saturated Fat: 2 g	

raspberry & pumpkin seed autumn salad

Bishop's Restaurant, Vancouver, BC

Nuts and seeds are high in fat but this is a "healthy" unsaturated fat, which has been shown to have a positive effect on the heart and blood pressure. Aim to substitute one of your meat portions for ¼ cup (60 mL) of seeds or nuts 4 to 5 times a week. The original recipe called just for raspberry vinegar but I added fresh raspberries to make the recipe healthier and increase the flavour. You could also dress up the salad by adding some mandarin orange slices and/or sliced strawberries.

Salad

8 cups (2 L) mixed autumn salad greens (any combination of arugula, curly endive, baby romaine, chervil, etc.)
½ cup (125 mL) toasted shelled pumpkin seeds

Raspberry vinaigrette

1 shallot, sliced
½ tsp (2 mL) Dijon mustard
½ cup (125 mL) raspberry vinegar
½ cup (125 mL) raspberries, fresh or defrosted and strained
1 tsp (5 mL) sugar
¼ cup (60 mL) grape seed oil
pepper to taste

For the salad: Divide greens onto 6 plates. To serve, drizzle raspberry vinaigrette (approximately 1 ½ tbsp / 20 mL per serving) over greens. Garnish with toasted pumpkin seeds.

Serves 6

For the vinaigrette: In a blender or food processor, process shallot, mustard, vinegar, raspberries and sugar until smooth. With blender running, add oil in a slow steady stream. Add pepper to taste.

Makes 1 cup (250 mL)

Nutrient Analysis per serving:

Calories: 87	Fibre: 1 g
Carbohydrates: 8 g	Cholesterol: 0 mg
Total fat: 6 g	Protein: 2 g
Potassium: 201 mg	Sodium: 15 mg
Saturated Fat: 1 g	

romaine salad with apple maple dressing

The Briars Inn and Country Club, Jackson's Point, ON

The original recipe, like most dressings, is high in fat. I reduced the oil and increased the vinegar; if you find it too vinegary, add a little bit of sugar. The apple in this dressing gives it a hint of sweetness. I also added a chopped apple to the salad for added texture and flavour.

Salad
1 large head romaine lettuce
1 cup (250 mL) cherry tomatoes, halved
½ English cucumber, sliced
5 mushrooms, thinly sliced
1 medium apple, cored and chopped

Apple maple dressing
1 apple, cored, peeled and chopped
⅓ cup (75 mL) apple juice
½ tbsp (7 mL) light mayonnaise
2 tbsp (30 mL) pure maple syrup
⅓ cup (75 mL) white wine vinegar
¼ cup (60 mL) olive oil
¼ tsp (1 mL) cilantro, chopped
pepper to taste

For the salad: Rinse, dry and tear romaine into bite-size pieces and arrange on 4 chilled salad plates. Top with cherry tomatoes, cucumber, mushrooms and apple just before serving. Drizzle with Apple Maple Dressing (approximately 1 tbsp / 15 mL per serving).

Serves 4

For the dressing: To prepare the dressing, combine all ingredients in a blender and purée at high speed until smooth. Refrigerate any leftover dressing in a jar for up to 1 week.

Makes 1 ½ cups (375 mL)

Nutrient Analysis per serving:

Calories: 130	Fibre: 5 g
Carbohydrates: 20 g	Cholesterol: 0 mg
Total fat: 6 g	Protein: 3 g
Potassium: 720 mg	Sodium: 22 mg
Saturated Fat: 1 g	

tomato and cucumber salad

Campbell House, Trinity, NL

The yogurt dressing on this salad is similar to the Greek tzatziki dip and makes a great healthy dressing. The original recipe called for regular sour cream and yogurt but, to cut back on the fat content without sacrificing the taste, I recommend fat-free yogurt and fat-free sour cream.

Salad
⅓ English cucumber, thinly sliced
1 large tomato, seeded and diced
1 head Romaine lettuce
2 wedges of lemon
fresh parsley to garnish

Yogurt mint dressing
½ cup (125 mL) fat-free plain yogurt
⅓ cup (75 mL) fat-free sour cream
1 tsp (5 mL) concentrated mint sauce
1 tbsp (15 mL) fresh parsley, chopped
pinch each of pepper and coriander

For the salad: Combine cucumber and tomato in a medium bowl. Pour yogurt mint dressing over mixture and stir. Refrigerate until ready to eat. To serve, chop lettuce and place in bowls. Spoon tomato mixture over lettuce and garnish with parsley and lemon wedges.

Serves 4 (or 2 generous servings)

For the dressing: In a small bowl combine yogurt, sour cream, mint sauce, chopped parsley, pepper and coriander. Mix until well-blended.

Makes ¾ cup (175 mL)

Nutrient Analysis per generous serving:

Calories: 166	Fibre: 9 g
Carbohydrates: 33 g	Cholesterol: 5 mg
Total fat: 1 g	Protein: 11 g
Potassium: 1464 mg	Sodium: 135 mg
Saturated Fat: 0 g	

insalata verde

Shadow Lawn Inn, Rothesay, NB

If you are unable to find fresh shelled peas, just add more of the other vegetables. This is a great summer salad; the citrus gives it a fresh taste. The dressing is best if you allow it to sit for several hours, but this is not necessary if time is an issue. I modified the recipe by cutting back on the oil and increasing the juices.

Salad

1 bunch of broccoli
½ lb (225 g) fresh green beans
1 bunch small asparagus
½ lb (225 g) snow peas
½ lb (225 g) fresh shelled peas
zest of 1 lemon, finely slivered

Citrus dressing

½ cup (125 mL) orange juice
¼ cup (60 mL) freshly squeezed lemon juice
2 tbsp (30 mL) sugar
¼ cup (60 mL) canola oil
1 tsp (5 mL) dried oregano
1 tsp (5 mL) dried marjoram

For the salad: Cut all vegetables into bite-size pieces, keeping the vegetables separated. Bring a large pot of water to a boil. As each of the vegetables is blanched, immediately remove to a bowl of ice water. Blanch broccoli and green beans for 2 to 3 minutes; asparagus for 1 minute; and snow peas and fresh peas for 30 seconds. Drain cooled vegetables and toss with lemon zest. Refrigerate until ready to use. To serve, toss chilled vegetables with dressing (approximately 1 ½ tbsp / 20 mL per serving) and arrange on individual plates.

Serves 6 to 8

For the dressing: In a small bowl, whisk together orange juice, lemon juice, sugar, oil, marjoram and oregano. Refrigerate leftover dressing.

Makes 1 cup (250 mL)

Nutrient Analysis per serving (based on 6):

Calories: 137	Fibre: 6 g
Carbohydrates: 20 g	Cholesterol: 0 mg
Total fat: 5 g	Protein: 6 g
Potassium: 618 mg	Sodium: 39 mg
Saturated Fat: 0 g	

cranberry and sunflower seed broccoli salad

The Murray Manor Bed and Breakfast, Yarmouth, NS

I made several changes to this recipe, including substituting fat-free sour cream and vinegar for a portion of the mayonnaise. The original recipe calls for candied ginger and raisins; I prefer it with dried cranberries, but you can customize it to your own liking.

2 large bunches fresh broccoli, cut into bite-sized florets
¼ cup (60 mL) dried cranberries
¼ cup (60 mL) sunflower seeds
¼ cup (60 mL) light mayonnaise
¼ cup (60 mL) fat-free sour cream
1 tbsp (15 mL) vinegar
1 tbsp (15 mL) sugar
pepper to taste

In a large bowl, combine broccoli, cranberries and sunflower seeds. In a small bowl, mix together mayonnaise, sour cream, vinegar, sugar and pepper. Pour mayonnaise mixture over broccoli to coat evenly.

Serves 6

Nutrient Analysis per serving:	
Calories: 149	Fibre: 6 g
Carbohydrates: 23 g	Cholesterol: 4 mg
Total fat: 6 g	Protein: 7 g
Potassium: 669 mg	Sodium: 143 mg
Saturated Fat: 1g	

warm scallop and portobello salad

The Schoolhouse Country Inn Restaurant, Belwood, ON

The juices from the scallops and mushrooms provide all the flavour in this salad. It is delicious served warm.

2 tsp (10 mL) olive oil
4 large portobello mushrooms, thinly sliced
1 clove garlic, minced
1 tbsp (15 mL) fresh ginger, minced
1 shallot, minced
3 tbsp (45 mL) water
¾ lb (340 g) large sea scallops, halved
¼ cup (60 mL) balsamic vinegar
8 cups (2 L) mixed salad greens
1 sprig fresh thyme
pepper to taste

In a skillet, heat oil over medium-high heat; sauté mushrooms, garlic, ginger and shallot until tender. Add water, scallops and balsamic vinegar; cover and cook until scallops are firm and opaque.

Arrange greens on 4 plates. Using a slotted spoon, remove scallops and mushrooms from skillet; place on top of greens. Stir thyme and pepper into liquid in skillet and simmer for several minutes. Drizzle over salad.

Serves 4

Nutrient Analysis per serving:

Calories: 149
Carbohydrates: 13 g
Total fat: 3 g
Potassium: 872 mg
Saturated Fat: 0 g

Fibre: 2 g
Cholesterol: 28 mg
Protein: 18 g
Sodium: 167 mg

curried lentil salad

This is one of my favorite salads; the curry adds a great flavour. Canned lentils are quick and convenient but also high in salt (sodium). If possible, I recommend preparing dried lentils for this recipe; although the sodium per serving using canned lentils is not significantly high, you can decrease it from 167 mg to 11 mg.

2 cups (500 mL) cooked lentils (from dried)*
½ cup (125 mL) diced red onion
1 ½ cups (375 mL) tomatoes, seeded and diced
1 cup (250 mL) fresh parsley, chopped
⅓ cup (75 mL) red wine vinegar
2 tbsp (30 mL) olive oil
1 clove garlic, minced
2 tsp (10 mL) curry powder
2 tsp (10 mL) granulated sugar
pepper to taste

In a large bowl combine lentils, red onion, tomatoes and parsley. In a small bowl combine vinegar, oil, garlic, curry powder and sugar. Pour dressing over lentil mixture and toss.

Serves 6

*To prepare lentils: Cover lentils with water in saucepan; bring to boil. Reduce heat to a simmer and cover. Cook until lentils are tender (varies from 30 minutes to 1 hour). Allow to cool and store extra in refrigerator or freezer.

Nutrient Analysis per serving:

Calories: 140	Fibre: 6 g
Carbohydrates: 18 g	Cholesterol: 0 g
Total fat: 5 g	Protein: 7 g
Potassium: 430 mg	Sodium: 11 mg
Saturated Fat: 1 g	

black bean and couscous salad

This salad is always a hit and very easy to prepare. You can enjoy it as a side or a light main dish. I've made it for my nutrition classes and everyone always loves it. Ideally it is best to use black beans prepared from dried rather than canned due to sodium (salt) content; however, if time is an issue use canned beans drained and rinsed well. Canned black beans do tend to be slightly lower in sodium compared to other varieties of canned beans. Make sure to check the nutritional information on labels: I came across one brand that contains 280 mg sodium per cup as opposed to 400 mg in another brand.

Salad

1 cup (250 mL) dry whole wheat couscous, prepared as per directions
½ cup (125 mL) red onion, diced
1 large tomato, seeded & diced
1 large green pepper, seeded & diced
¾ cup (175 mL) frozen corn kernels, thawed
2 cups (500 mL) black beans or turtle beans, drained & rinsed

Dressing

juice from 1 lime
¼ cup (60 mL) red wine vinegar
2 tbsp (30 mL) olive oil
1 tsp (5 mL) cumin
1 tsp (5 mL) sugar

For the salad: In a large bowl, combine onion, tomato, green pepper, corn and black beans with couscous. Pour dressing over couscous and toss until well combined.

Serves 6

For the dressing: Mix together lime juice, vinegar, oil, cumin and sugar.

Makes ⅓ cup (100 mL)

Nutrient Analysis per serving:

Calories: 269
Carbohydrates: 46 g
Total fat: 5 g
Potassium: 535 mg
Saturated Fat: 1 g
Fibre: 8 g
Cholesterol: 0 mg
Protein: 10 g
Sodium: 10 mg

chickpea and sun-dried tomato salad with roasted red pepper dressing

Although canned chickpeas are convenient, they are high in salt. I recommend planning ahead and preparing dried chickpeas (along with other legumes) to have on hand. If canned chickpeas are all you have, make sure to always drain and rinse well. Sun-dried tomatoes are also high in sodium, but you only need a small amount to get the flavour. If time is an issue you can purchase red peppers already roasted.

Salad

1 head romaine lettuce, washed and cut into bite-size pieces
1 large red pepper, thinly sliced
½ cup (125 mL) mushrooms, thinly sliced
¼ cup (60 mL) sun-dried tomatoes, thinly sliced
2 cups (500 mL) cooked chickpeas* (or 1 can (19oz / 540 mL
   chickpeas), drained and rinsed

Roasted red pepper dressing

1 large red pepper, roasted** (or ½ cup (125 mL) roasted red peppers)
1 clove garlic, chopped
¼ cup (60 mL) balsamic vinegar
2 tbsp (30 mL) light sour cream
1 tbsp (15 mL) fresh basil leaves
1 tbsp (15 mL) olive oil

For the salad: In a large bowl combine lettuce, red pepper, mushrooms, sun-dried tomatoes and chickpeas. Toss salad with ½ cup dressing and serve.

Serves 4

For the dressing: Combine roasted red pepper, garlic, balsamic vinegar, sour cream and basil in a blender and process until smooth. With blender running, add oil in a slow steady stream.

Makes ¾ cup (175 mL)

*To prepare dried legumes: soak in unsalted water overnight, drain and rinse. Place in a large saucepan of water and bring to a boil. Simmer until tender, about 1 hour. Cool, then store in refrigerator or freezer.

Yield: 1 cup (250 mL) dried = 2 ¼ cups (550 mL) cooked.

**To roast peppers: Cut pepper in half, remove seeds, and place cut side down on a baking sheet; broil until blackened. When cooled, remove skins.

Nutrient Analysis per serving:

Calories: 252	Fibre: 11 g
Carbohydrates: 37 g	Cholesterol: 5 mg
Total fat: 8 g	Protein: 11 g
Potassium: 932 mg	Sodium: 106 mg
Saturated Fat: 2 g	

exotic spinach salad

Beild House, Collingwood, ON

The exotic fruit is a great complement to this spinach salad and is also rich in potassium, a mineral that has a positive effect on blood pressure. Choose a combination of recommended fruits listed below.

Salad

12 cups (3 L) fresh spinach leaves
1 cup (250 mL) sliced fruit (combination of mandarin oranges, strawberries, kiwis, grapefruit, mangoes or papaya)
¼ cup (60 mL) slivered almonds (preferably toasted*)

Sweet poppy seed dressing

¼ cup (60 mL) raspberry balsamic vinegar
2 tbsp (30 mL) granulated sugar
1 tbsp (15 mL) poppy seeds
¼ tsp (1 mL) paprika
2 tsp (10 mL) onion, minced
¼ tsp (1 mL) Worcestershire sauce
¼ cup (60 mL) water
¼ cup (60 mL) vegetable oil

For the salad: In a large bowl, combine spinach, fruit and almonds just before serving. Toss salad with dressing (approximately ¾ cup / 175 mL) and serve.

Serves 6

*To quickly toast almonds, sauté on medium heat in a non-stick skillet.

For the dressing: In a small bowl, stir the vinegar and sugar together; microwave on high for 30 seconds to break down the sugar crystals. In a blender, process vinegar and sugar mixture, poppy seeds, paprika, onion, Worcestershire sauce and water for 30 seconds. With blender running, add vegetable oil in a slow steady stream, blending until emulsified.

Makes 1 cup (250 mL)

Nutrient Analysis per serving:	
Calories: 135	Fibre: 3 g
Carbohydrates: 12 g	Cholesterol: 0 mg
Total fat: 9 g	Protein: 3 g
Potassium: 457 mg	Sodium: 52 mg
Saturated Fat: 0 g	

seafood pasta salad

Billy's Seafood Company, Saint John, NB

I made this recipe healthier by adding vegetables and substituting fat-free plain yogurt for some of the mayonnaise. It is also delicious thrown over greens. Enjoy it as a main course or as a side; if you choose to have it as a side, cut back on the protein portion of your meal.

Salad

3 cups (750 mL) dry whole wheat rotini
1 large green pepper, sliced
1 medium tomato, seeded and diced
¼ lb (125 g) cooked small scallops (80–100 count)
¼ lb (125 g) cooked salad shrimp (110–130 count)
fresh parsley, as garnish

Honey Dijon dressing

2 tbsp (30 mL) Dijon mustard
2 tbsp (30 mL) light mayonnaise
2 tbsp (30 mL) fat-free plain yogurt
2 tbsp (30 mL) liquid honey

For the salad: In a large saucepan, cook pasta al dente as per directions on box, omitting any recommended salt or oil. Drain, rinse with cold water and thoroughly drain again. Mix in sliced pepper, tomato, scallops and shrimp. Toss with dressing to coat. Sprinkle with parsley.

Serves 4 as meal (or 8 as side)

For the dressing: In a small bowl, whisk together mustard, mayonnaise, yogurt and honey.

Makes ½ cup (125 mL)

Nutrient Analysis per serving as side:

Calories: 137	Fibre: 2 g
Carbohydrates: 21 g	Cholesterol: 36 mg
Total fat: 2 g	Protein: 10 g
Potassium: 217 mg	Sodium: 159 mg
Saturated Fat: 0 g	

FISH & SEAFOOD

the ledges pasta with shrimp and scallops, p.28

roasted roma tomatoes with scallops, p.35

HOLD THE SALT, NOT THE SEAFOOD!

Fish and seafood are recommended for at least 2-3 meals a week. Not only do they provide a source of protein, B vitamins and iron but also a heart-healthy fat called omega-3 fatty acids. Research has shown that omega-3 may play a role in regulating blood pressure, lowering 'bad' cholesterol while increasing 'good' cholesterol, as well as improving blood circulation. The majority of fish and seafood provide some omega-3 but, fattier fish — salmon, trout, herring, mackerel — are the richest sources. Omega-3 is also found in other foods including walnuts, flax, soy, and omega-3 enhanced eggs.

Eating more fish and seafood is easy when there are so many versatile ways of preparing it. If you are craving pasta, try either of the potassium rich dishes: the Ledges Pasta with Shrimp and Scallops or the Quaco Inn Lobster and Pasta. For a healthier and tastier alternative to tartar sauce, the Creamy Roasted Red Pepper Tilapia adds a lot of flavour to a milder tasting fish. The Grilled Salmon Fillet with Summer Salsa is a fresh tasting dish that can be enjoyed any time of the year.

grilled salmon fillet with summer salsa, p.34

the ledges pasta with shrimp and scallops

The Ledges Inn, Doaktown, NB

This is a simple and delicious meal. The original recipe called just for shrimp but I cut back on the portion (due to high cholesterol content) and added scallops. The cholesterol in this recipe is still high, so if you have concerns with your cholesterol levels, I would suggest omitting the shrimp and increasing the amount of scallops. The recipe also called for lemon pepper linguine but I substituted whole wheat pasta and it's still very flavourful. Many canned tomato sauces are high in sodium; using canned diced tomatoes with no added salt works very well and adds texture.

Pasta sauce

1 tsp (5 mL) olive oil

1 medium onion, diced

2 cloves garlic, minced

1 tsp (5 mL) fresh sage (¼ tsp / 1 mL dried)

1 ½ cups (375 mL) canned diced tomatoes with no added salt

⅓ cup (75 mL) red wine

1 tbsp (15 mL) non-hydrogenated soft margarine

1 tbsp (15 mL) freshly squeezed lemon juice

dried chili flakes to taste (optional)

3–4 drops Tabasco sauce

Shrimp and scallops

5 oz (150 g) medium shrimp, raw, peeled and deveined

7 oz (200 g) scallops, raw

2 tsp (10 mL) olive oil

flour for dredging

3 cups (750 mL) cooked whole wheat linguine, prepared as per directions

For the sauce: Heat oil in a large skillet; add and sauté onion, garlic and sage until tender, approximately 2 to 3 minutes. Stir in tomatoes, wine, margarine, lemon juice, chili flakes and Tabasco sauce; simmer 3 to 4 minutes. Set aside and keep warm.

For the shrimp and scallops: While sauce is cooking, dredge shrimp and scallops in flour and quickly pan-fry in olive oil, tossing frequently until done, about 4 minutes. Shrimp will turn pink and become firm, and scallops will become opaque and firm. Do not overcook.

To serve, divide linguine onto 4 serving plates. Top with shrimp and scallops and drizzle with sauce.

Serves 4

Nutrient Analysis per serving:

Calories: 302	Fibre: 6 g
Carbohydrates: 37 g	Cholesterol: 69 mg
Total fat: 7 g	Protein: 22 g
Potassium: 514 mg	Sodium: 172 mg
Saturated Fat: 1 g	

citrus and maple glazed salmon fillets

Severn River Inn, Severn Bridge, ON

*The original recipe had two separate steps, a marinade for
the fish and a maple glaze cooked separately and added
to the fish once cooked. To cut back on preparation time,
I combined the ingredients to make one marinade. I also
decreased the salmon portions and the amount of oil and
maple syrup to cut back on the fat and overall calories. If
you are unable to marinate the fish beforehand, combine
all ingredients and cook the fish in the sauce, although the
cooking time may need to be increased.*

2 tsp (10 mL) olive oil
2 tsp (10 mL) chili powder
1 tsp (5 mL) fresh ginger
1 small clove garlic, minced
juice from ½ lemon
juice from ½ lime
juice from ½ orange
¼ cup (60 mL) pure maple syrup
pinch of pepper
6 salmon fillets (3 oz / 85 g each), skin removed
fresh cilantro for garnish (optional)

Combine oil, chili powder, ginger, garlic, citrus juices, maple
syrup and pepper in a large re-sealable plastic bag. Place
fish in bag and coat. Marinate in the refrigerator for several
hours. When ready to prepare, preheat oven to 350°F
(180°C). Remove fillets from bag, place in a baking dish
and bake for 8 to 10 minutes or until fish flakes easily when
tested with a fork. Garnish with cilantro and serve.

Serves 6

Nutrient Analysis per serving:

Calories: 175	Fibre: 0 g
Carbohydrates: 11 g	Cholesterol: 47 mg
Total fat: 7 g	Protein: 17 g
Potassium: 471 mg	Sodium: 39 mg
Saturated Fat: 1 g	

creamy roasted red pepper tilapia

Tilapia is a lean, low-fat white fish that is quite versatile. It has a mild taste, so this roasted red pepper sauce is a great way to add some flavour. Red peppers can be purchased pre-roasted or you can roast them yourself (see p. 22).

Tilapia
1 lb (500 g) tilapia fillets
juice from 1 lemon
pepper to taste

Creamy roasted red pepper sauce
¾ cup (175 mL) roasted red pepper, diced
2 tbsp (30 mL) light mayonnaise
2 tbsp (30 mL) light sour cream
1 tsp (5 mL) lemon juice
3 tbsp (45 mL) chopped shallots

For the tilapia: Place fish on a lightly-greased pan; sprinkle fish with lemon juice and pepper. Broil for about 6 to 8 minutes or until fish is opaque and flakes easily when tested with a fork. Serve fish topped with red pepper sauce and shallots.

Serves 6

For the sauce: In a small bowl, combine red peppers, mayonnaise, sour cream, lemon juice and shallots.

Nutrient Analysis per serving:

Calories: 121	Fibre: 0 g
Carbohydrates: 3 mg	Cholesterol: 41 mg
Total fat: 4 g	Protein: 15 g
Potassium: 288 mg	Sodium: 86 mg
Saturated Fat: 0 g	

quaco inn lobster and pasta

Quaco Inn, St. Martins, NB

Fresh herbs always taste better than dried but whatever you have on hand can be used. If you have high cholesterol you should watch your dietary cholesterol intake but, more importantly, limit your fat intake because it has more of a negative effect on blood cholesterol levels. Seafood provides many heart-healthy nutrients but does contain cholesterol — lobster being one of the higher sources. Despite this, lobster is so delicious, I think everyone should enjoy this delicacy even in moderation; therefore there is only a small portion of lobster in this dish.

2 tsp (10 mL) olive oil
2–3 garlic cloves, minced
½ lb (225 g) lobster meat, in bite-sized pieces
1 tbsp (15 mL) chopped fresh basil (or 1 tsp / 5 mL dried)
1 tbsp (15 mL) chopped fresh chives (or 1 tsp / 5 mL dried)
2–3 medium tomatoes, cut in wedges
19-oz (540-mL) can low-sodium tomatoes (Italian-style plum or diced)
zest and juice of 1 lime
pepper to taste
¼ cup (60 mL) freshly grated Parmesan cheese
3 cups (750 mL) whole wheat pasta, cooked al dente and drained

Heat oil in a heavy-bottomed saucepan, add garlic and sauté until fragrant, being careful not to brown. Add lobster and sauté until heated through. Add herbs, fresh and canned tomatoes, lime juice and zest. Season with pepper. Stir in Parmesan cheese and return to serving temperature.
Serve lobster sauce over pasta; garnish with fresh herbs and a small sprinkle of Parmesan, if desired.

Serves 4

Nutrient Analysis per serving:	
Calories: 285	Fibre: 7 g
Carbohydrates: 40 g	Cholesterol: 45 mg
Total fat: 6 g	Protein: 22 g
Potassium: 650 mg	Sodium: 216 mg
Saturated Fat: 2 g	

grilled salmon fillet with summer salsa

The Latch Country Inn, Sidney, BC

Summer salsa is a nutritious accompaniment to salmon. Capers are usually quite high in sodium, so limit the amount you use. This makes a fair amount of salsa so either load it up on the salmon or enjoy it as a tomato side salad. Tomatoes are known for their antioxidant properties, especially one in particular called lycopene, and are also rich in potassium. Both nutrients have been shown to have a beneficial effect on blood pressure and have anti-cancer properties.

Salmon

4 salmon fillets (3 oz / 85 g each), skin removed
2 tbsp (30 mL) fresh lemon juice
pepper to taste

Summer salsa

1 tbsp (15 mL) olive oil
¼ cup (60 mL) minced shallots
1 tbsp (15 mL) lemon zest
2 tbsp (30 mL) lemon juice
12 oz (340 g) cherry tomatoes, quartered
½ English cucumber, diced
¼ cup (60 mL) diced red onion
½ large yellow pepper, diced
1 tbsp (15 mL) capers, drained
1 tbsp (15 mL) chopped cilantro

For the salmon: Brush salmon with lemon juice and sprinkle with pepper. Place in an ovenproof baking dish and bake at 400°F (200°C) for 6 to 8 minutes or until salmon is opaque and flakes easily. To serve, spoon Summer Salsa over salmon.

Serves 4

For the salsa: In a small bowl, whisk together oil, shallots, lemon zest and juice until well blended. In a large bowl, combine tomatoes, cucumber, onion, yellow pepper, capers and cilantro; pour dressing over mixture and stir to combine.

Makes 4 to 5 cups

Nutrient Analysis per serving:

Calories: 225	Fibre: 2 g
Carbohydrates: 10 g	Cholesterol: 47 mg
Total fat: 13 g	Protein: 19 g
Potassium: 826 mg	Sodium: 107 mg
Saturated Fat: 2 g	

roasted roma tomatoes with scallops

Lake Louise Station, Lake Louise, AB

The combination of juices from the scallops and tomatoes provide great flavour, and I was able to cut back on the oil without sacrificing the taste. This can be served over salad greens if you want a light meal or over whole wheat pasta for something more filling.

6 small Roma tomatoes
¾ lb (375 g) sea scallops
2 tbsp (30 mL) olive oil
2 shallots, diced
1 large clove garlic, minced
ground pepper to taste
¼ cup (60 mL) balsamic vinegar
2 tbsp (30 mL) sliced black olives (kalamata)
6–8 cups (1.5–2 L) mesclun salad greens
fresh basil leaves for garnish

Slice tomatoes in half and scoop out seeds and membrane with a teaspoon. If necessary, take a small sliver off bottom so that tomatoes will balance on a plate. Invert onto paper towel and set aside.

Rinse scallops and pat dry. Heat 1 tbsp (15 mL) oil in a non-stick skillet over medium heat and sauté shallots, garlic and scallops until scallops are partially cooked, about 3 minutes. Season with pepper. Remove scallops and set aside. Add balsamic vinegar to pan and remove from heat.

Preheat oven to 375°F (190°C). Place tomato halves in a shallow baking dish; stuff with scallops and olives. Drizzle tomatoes with remaining oil. Bake for 10 minutes. Serve on a bed of mesclun salad greens; drizzle with reserved balsamic mixture and garnish with fresh basil leaves.

Serves 4

Nutrient Analysis per serving:

Calories: 110	Fibre: 1 g
Carbohydrates: 8 g	Cholesterol: 28 mg
Total fat: 1 g	Protein: 15 g
Potassium: 436 mg	Sodium: 190 mg
Saturated Fat: 0 g	

trout baked in apple cider

Langdon Hall, Cambridge, ON

Apple gives this dish a nice fruity flavour. Trout has a nutritional value similar to salmon, providing a source of heart-healthy omega-3 fatty acids. To cut back on preparation time, purchase a bag of pre-sliced carrots and use approximately ½ cup (125 mL).

1 medium onion, cut into ⅛-in (0.3-cm) slices
1 carrot, cut into ⅛-in (0.3-cm) slices
4 trout fillets (3 oz / 85 g each), skin removed
1 cup (250 mL) apple cider
pepper to taste
¼ cup (60 mL) cider vinegar
1 ½ tbsp (22 mL) liquid honey
2 tbsp (30 mL) light cream (5% m. f.)

In a medium microwave-safe bowl, microwave carrot and onion for 5 to 7 minutes, until tender. Place fish in a lightly greased non-stick baking dish. Top with carrot, onion, apple cider and pepper; cover dish with foil. Preheat oven to 400°F (200°C) and bake for 8 to 10 minutes or until fish is opaque and flakes easily when tested with a fork.

Pour half the juice from the fish into a small saucepan and add cider vinegar; cook over high heat until boiling, approximately 4 minutes. Add honey and cream and boil again for 2 minutes. Spoon sauce over trout to serve.

Serves 4

Nutrient Analysis per serving:	
Calories: 219	Fibre: 1 g
Carbohydrates: 15 g	Cholesterol: 53 mg
Total fat: 9 g	Protein: 18 g
Potassium: 416 mg	Sodium: 61 mg
Saturated Fat: 2 g	

creamy sweet curried sea scallops

Restaurant Le Caveau, Grand Pré, NS

The combination of scallops, fruit and curry makes this dish a delight. Serve it with brown rice and a side vegetable of choice. I significantly cut back on the fat content by reducing the butter/margarine and replacing the heavy cream with fat-free yogurt and sour cream. There are many different varieties of reduced-sodium broths that still contain a significant amount of salt; look for broths labelled "low in sodium." Serve this dish with a green salad and a slice of whole wheat French bread or brown rice.

Scallops

¾ lb (350 g) scallops
flour for dusting
1 medium banana, sliced

Curry sauce

1 ½ tbsp (22 mL) non-hydrogenated soft margarine
1 medium apple, peeled, cored and diced
½ small onion, diced
1 small banana, sliced
1 tbsp (15 mL) curry powder
3 tbsp (45 mL) white wine
½ cup (125 mL) low-sodium chicken stock
2 tbsp (30 mL) fat-free plain yogurt
2 tbsp (30 mL) fat-free sour cream
pepper to taste

For the scallops: Rinse scallops and pat dry. Dredge in flour, shaking off excess and sauté in a lightly oiled pan. Serve scallops with warm curry sauce and garnished with banana slices.

Serves 4

For the curry sauce: In a medium saucepan, melt margarine; sauté apples, onion and banana for 2 minutes, stirring often. Sprinkle with curry powder and continue to sauté for 1 minute. Stir in wine and chicken stock and bring to a full boil. Remove from heat and stir in yogurt and sour cream. Add pepper to taste.

Nutrient Analysis per serving:

Calories: 126	Fibre: 2 g
Carbohydrates: 21 g	Cholesterol: 28 mg
Total fat: 6 g	Protein: 16 g
Potassium: 674 mg	Sodium: 180 mg
Saturated Fat: 1 g	

halibut with beet relish

Aqua, St. John's, NL

The recipe calls for halibut but I tried it with a variety of white fish and it cooks well with all of them. To save time but not sacrifice flavour, I used pickled beets instead of baked fresh beets, then cut back on the vinegar and sugar. I also cooked the beet relish in the microwave instead of cooking it over the stove. Always check the labels to find the pickled beets with the lowest sodium content and, if possible, use homemade pickled beets without the added salt.

Beet relish

¾ cup (175 mL) pickled beets, finely chopped
¾ cup (175 mL) cabbage, finely chopped
1 cup (250 mL) apples, peeled and finely chopped
¼ cup (60 mL) apple cider vinegar
2 tbsp (30 mL) granulated sugar
½ tsp (2 mL) pepper
2 tsp (10 mL) whole-grain mustard

Halibut

4 portions halibut fillets (3 oz / 85 g each)
flour for dredging
2 tsp (10 mL) olive oil
1 shallot, finely chopped

For the relish: Combine beets, cabbage, apple and vinegar in a medium microwave-safe bowl. Microwave on high for 10 minutes, stirring halfway through. When cabbage is tender, remove from microwave and drain. Add sugar, pepper and mustard; stir well.

For the halibut: While beet relish is cooking, pat fish dry and lightly coat it with flour. In a non-stick skillet heat oil and shallot over medium-high heat. Add fish and cook for 10 to 12 minutes, until halibut is just done. Top halibut with beet relish.

Serves 4

Nutrient Analysis per serving:	
Calories: 188	Fibre: 2 g
Carbohydrates: 18 g	Cholesterol: 27 mg
Total fat: 4 g	Protein: 19 g
Potassium: 529 mg	Sodium: 191 mg
Saturated Fat: 1 g	

VEGETARIAN

hummus & vegetable pita pizza, p.44

grilled vegetable pita pockets with creamy dill mayo, p.51

HOLD THE SALT — AND TRY THESE VEGETARIAN MAINS!

Vegetarian dishes are becoming more and more popular although many folks still find it hard to incorporate meatless meals into their weekly menu on a regular basis. Studies show that vegetarians tend to have lower rates of high blood pressure along with less obesity, heart disease and cancer. They tend to consume less saturated fat, and have a diet richer in fruits, vegetables and fibre. This does not mean you need to cut out animal products, but just aim to incorporate at least one meatless meal a week.

Choosing a healthy vegetarian dish can start here…. I guarantee if going meatless is a difficult adjustment, these are the dishes to change your mind. Try the juicy and flavourful Portobello Veggie Burgers or the tasty Grilled Vegetable Pita Pockets with Creamy Dill Mayo or the Dunes' Thai Chickpea Linguine. Chickpeas provide a great source of fibre and protein without the fat.

parmesan vegetarian zucchini bake, p.43

the dunes' thai chickpea linguine

The Dunes, Brackley Beach, PEI

The original recipe calls for shrimp, but when I tried it with chickpeas I thought it made a great vegetarian dish. Shrimp is very high in cholesterol so it's important to limit how often you have it. Canned chickpeas contain around 400 mg of sodium per cup, so I recommend planning in advance and cooking dried chickpeas (see p. 22 for method). If you have to use canned, be sure to drain and rinse chickpeas well.

Chickpeas and linguine
½ tbsp (7 mL) sesame oil
4 green onions, chopped
1 red pepper, thinly sliced
4 plum tomatoes, diced
2 cloves garlic, minced
2 cups (500 mL) cooked chickpeas
3 cups (750 mL) cooked whole wheat linguine prepared as per directions
fresh lime juice (optional)

Thai peanut sauce
1 garlic clove, minced
1 tbsp (15 mL) reduced-sodium soy sauce
⅓ cup (75 mL) creamy peanut butter
½ tbsp (7 mL) brown sugar
¾ cups (175 mL) water
1 tsp (5 mL) crushed chilis, or to taste

For the chickpeas and linguine: Heat sesame oil in a large skillet over medium heat; sauté onions, peppers, tomatoes and garlic for 2 minutes, stirring frequently. Add chickpeas and toss for 2 to 3 minutes. Pour Thai peanut sauce over vegetables and chickpeas in frying pan, stir in pasta and return to serving temperature. Squeeze lime juice over pasta for added flavour.

Serves 4

For the sauce: Combine all ingredients in a medium microwave-safe bowl; microwave on high for 1 minute.

Nutrient Analysis per serving:

Calories: 394	Fibre: 13 g
Carbohydrates: 62 g	Cholesterol: 0 mg
Total fat: 11 g	Protein: 18 g
Potassium: 622 mg	Sodium: 168 mg
Saturated Fat: 2 g	

parmesan vegetarian zucchini bake

Salmon River House Country Inn, Salmon River, NS

This is a simple, easy-to-prepare dish. Enjoy it as a light main meal served with a slice of whole wheat French bread and curried lentil salad (p. 20). I cut back on the fat by using light cheese and reducing the added oil. Prepared breadcrumbs can be high in sodium, so check the label or quickly prepare your own by processing several slices of bread in the food processor.

1 tsp (5 mL) canola oil
1 garlic clove, minced
5 small or 4 medium-sized zucchinis, cut into ¼-in (5-mm) slices
1 small onion, diced
5 medium tomatoes, seeded and diced in ¼-in (5-mm) cubes
1 ½ tsp (7 mL) each of sweet basil and oregano
pepper to taste
¼ cup (60 mL) Parmesan cheese, grated
½ cup (125 mL) whole wheat breadcrumbs
1 ½ tbsp (22 mL) non-hydrogenated soft margarine
⅓ cup (75 mL) light mozzarella cheese, grated

In a non-stick skillet, heat oil. Add garlic and sauté until fragrant. Add zucchini and sauté until it is browned and slightly transparent. Remove zucchini and reserve. Add onion, tomatoes and seasoning to skillet and sauté for several minutes until vegetables are softened.

Grease an 8-cup (2-L) casserole dish or spring pan. Place alternating layers of zucchini and tomatoes in the dish, sprinkling each layer with Parmesan and ending with tomatoes and Parmesan. Mix breadcrumbs with margarine and mozzarella and sprinkle over top. Bake in a preheated 350°F (180°C) oven for 30 minutes, until golden and bubbly. If time allows, let set for 15 to 20 minutes prior to serving.

Serves 6

Nutrient Analysis per serving:	
Calories: 126	Fibre: 4 g
Carbohydrates: 14 g	Cholesterol: 6 mg
Total fat: 6 g	Protein: 6 g
Potassium: 636 mg	Sodium: 168 mg
Saturated Fat: 2 g	

hummus & vegetable pita pizza

Hummus is a healthy Lebanese spread made from chickpeas. It provides a source of fibre, protein and potassium. Enjoy as a spread on sandwiches or pizzas, or as a dip with vegetables, crackers or pita bread. To save on time, you can purchase already prepared hummus but making it from scratch is quite easy and healthier, especially if you start by cooking dried chickpeas instead of using canned. (See page 22 for preparation method.)

Pita pizza

4 whole wheat pita breads, 7 in (18 cm) in diameter
½ cup (125 mL) hummus
2 tsp (10 mL) vegetable oil
1 red pepper, cut into thin strips
1 green pepper, cut into thin strips
3 green onions, chopped
6 mushrooms, thinly sliced
¼ cup (60 mL) grated Parmesan cheese
chopped cilantro, to taste

Hummus

2 cups (500 mL) chickpeas
2–3 cloves garlic
1 tbsp (15 mL) tahini or peanut butter
2 tbsp (30 mL) lemon juice
¼ cup (60 mL) fat-free plain yogurt
pepper to taste

For the pizza: In oven, broil pita bread on each side for several minutes until crispy (check frequently to avoid burning). Place pitas on a baking pan; spread 2 tablespoons of hummus on top of each pita. Heat oil in a non-stick skillet over medium-high heat. Add vegetables and sauté until tender, approximately 4 minutes; remove from heat. Top pita with sautéed vegetables, followed by grated cheese. Return to oven and broil for 4 to 5 minutes or until heated through. Garnish with cilantro.

Serves 4

For the hummus: Blend all ingredients in a food processor until smooth.

Nutrient Analysis per serving:

Calories: 219	Fibre: 5 g
Carbohydrates: 32 g	Cholesterol: 0 mg
Total fat: 6 g	Protein: 9 g
Potassium: 605 mg	Sodium: 225 mg
Saturated Fat: 1 g	

mexican black bean fajitas

You won't even miss the meat in this dish. Black beans are used in many Mexican dishes, including fajitas and quesadillas. Without alterations to this dish, the sodium content would be quite high. I recommend planning in advance and cooking dried black beans, due to the high sodium content in canned beans. If you use canned beans, check labels and choose the ones with the lowest sodium content; be sure to drain and rinse well. Prepared tortilla breads are also high in sodium; instead, make your own whole wheat tortillas (omitting the salt), or use pita bread or corn tortillas softened in a skillet or in the microwave. Serve fajitas with a side salad of your choice.

2 cloves garlic, minced
1 tsp (5 mL) vegetable oil
1 medium red pepper, cut into thin strips
1 medium green pepper, cut into thin strips
1 medium onion, thinly sliced
8 mushrooms, sliced
1 medium tomato, chopped
2 cups (500 mL) cooked black beans
½ tbsp (7 mL) chili powder
pinch cayenne (optional)
12 small corn tortillas
condiments: salsa, light sour cream, light cheddar cheese

Heat garlic and oil in a large non-stick skillet over medium-high heat until fragrant. Add red and green peppers, onion and mushrooms and sauté for several minutes until slightly tender, about 4 minutes. Add black beans, tomato, chili powder and cayenne and continue to cook until warmed through. If corn tortillas are firm, place on a skillet over medium heat for 30 seconds to soften. Spread ½ tablespoon each of salsa, sour cream and cheese on each tortilla, followed by vegetable–bean mixture; roll up by tucking up one end and folding in each side.

Serves 6 (2 fajitas per serving)

Nutrient Analysis per serving:

Calories: 234	Fibre: 7 g
Carbohydrates: 40 g	Cholesterol: 8 mg
Total fat: 5 g	Protein: 11 g
Potassium: 651 mg	Sodium: 163 mg
Saturated Fat: 2 g	

frittata trattoria

Trattoria Di Umberto Restaurant, Whistler, BC

This is a simple and delicious Italian omelette. The goat cheese gives it a great flavour, differing from the traditional cheddar cheese. I used only egg whites to significantly decrease the cholesterol content. To save on time, I omitted roasting the red pepper and cooking the omelette in the oven. If you prefer, you can use roasted red peppers but I found sautéing the peppers still brought out the flavour.

12 egg whites
1 tbsp (15 mL) chopped fresh basil or ½ tsp (2 mL) dried basil
pepper to taste
1 tsp (5 mL) olive oil
1 red pepper, chopped
½ cup (125 mL) button or cremini mushrooms, sliced
¼ cup (60 mL) goat cheese

In a large bowl, beat together egg whites, basil and pepper; set aside.

Heat oil in a non-stick skillet over medium heat. Sauté red pepper and mushrooms for 4 minutes. Stir in egg mixture and goat cheese. Cook for 3-4 minutes, then flip omelette to finish cooking on the other side. Remove from skillet and serve.

Serves 4

Nutrient Analysis per serving:

Calories: 92	Fibre: 1 g
Carbohydrates: 4 g	Cholesterol: 3 mg
Total fat: 3 g	Protein: 13 g
Potassium: 294 mg	Sodium: 192 mg
Saturated Fat: 1 g	

portobello veggie burgers

Elaine Elliot and Virginia Lee

I guarantee that everyone — those who prefer vegetarian meals and meat lovers alike — will enjoy these burgers. Compared to typical beef burgers, these are lower in saturated fat and high in potassium. I cut back on the oil to decrease the fat and calorie content. In order for this recipe to be quick, I eliminated the 2-hour marinating time but, because Portobellos are so flavourful and juicy, this healthier, quicker version turned out to be delicious.

8 Portobello mushroom caps, 4–5 in (7.5–10 cm) in diameter
2 tbsp (30 mL) olive oil
¼ cup (60 mL) balsamic vinegar
1 tbsp (15 mL) garlic, minced
2 tbsp (30 mL) fresh thyme leaves, chopped
8 whole wheat hamburger buns
assorted condiments:
lettuce
tomato slices
green or red pepper slices
½ an avocado, thinly sliced

Remove stems from mushrooms and carefully wipe the caps with a damp cloth. In a bowl, whisk together olive oil, balsamic vinegar, garlic and thyme until well blended. Place caps in bowl with vinegar mixture and turn to coat. Preheat grill* to medium heat. Place caps on grill and cook for 6 to 8 minutes, turning once, until mushrooms are cooked. Serve immediately on toasted buns with condiments of choice.

Serves 8

*Grilling is the preferred method but these can also be prepared in a skillet on the stove; you may need to add some of the vinegar mixture if you find it is dry.

Nutrient Analysis per serving:	
Calories: 179	Fibre: 4 g
Carbohydrates: 28 g	Cholesterol: 0 mg
Total fat: 5 g	Protein: 7 g
Potassium: 654 mg	Sodium: 208 mg
Saturated Fat: 1 g	

vegetable medley stir-fry

Shaw's Hotel, Brackley Beach, PEI

A little bit of sesame oil goes a long way, giving any dish that delicious Asian flavour. Choose from a variety of different vegetables according to your preference. This stir-fry can be served as a side dish or as a main course. Reduced-sodium soy sauces usually remain high in salt but brands vary significantly, so always check labels for the healthiest option. I prefer fresh vegetables but to cut down on preparation time, you can use frozen mixed vegetables.

2 tsp (10 mL) vegetable oil
1 medium onion, cut into wedges
1 clove garlic, minced
1 head broccoli, cut into bite-sized florets
1 head cauliflower, cut into bite-sized florets
1 small zucchini, sliced
½ tbsp (7 mL) reduced-sodium soy sauce
1 tsp (5 mL) lemon pepper
½ tsp (2 mL) sesame oil
2 medium tomatoes, cut into wedges
2–3 cups (500 mL–750 mL) cooked instant brown rice
1 tbsp (15 mL) sesame seeds, toasted*

Heat oil in a wok or large skillet over medium heat. Add onion and garlic; stir-fry until onion starts to soften. Add broccoli and cauliflower and stir-fry about 2 minutes. Add zucchini and cook an additional 2 minutes, until crisp-tender. Stir in soy sauce, lemon pepper and sesame oil. Add tomato wedges and cook 1 minute. Serve over brown rice and sprinkle with toasted sesame seeds.

Serves 4

*To toast sesame seeds: sauté over medium heat in a non-stick skillet until slightly golden.

Nutrient Analysis per serving:

Calories: 292	Fibre: 12 g
Carbohydrates: 53 g	Cholesterol: 0 mg
Total fat: 6 g	Protein: 12 g
Potassium: 1292 mg	Sodium: 169 mg
Saturated Fat: 1 g	

grilled vegetable pita pockets with creamy dill mayo

Elaine Elliot and Virginia Lee

If you don't have a grill to cook the vegetables, roast them in the oven instead. This still brings out the flavour. I substituted light mayonnaise and fat-free plain yogurt for the full-fat versions and the result was just as tasty. Serve this pita with Herb and Garlic Roasted Mini Potatoes (p. 73).

Grilled vegetables

1 ½ tbsp (22 mL) olive oil (preferably herb or citrus-infused)
1 medium eggplant, sliced lengthwise ¼ in (5 mm) thick
2 medium zucchini, sliced lengthwise ¼ in (5 mm) thick
1 sweet red pepper, cut in strips
1 sweet yellow pepper, cut in strips
pepper to taste
4 whole-wheat pita breads, 7 in (18 cm) in diameter

Dill mayo

¼ cup (60 mL) light mayonnaise
⅓ cup (75 mL) fat-free plain yogurt
2 tsp (10 mL) grated onion
1 tbsp (15 mL) chopped fresh dill or ¾ tsp (4 mL) dried dill weed

For the vegetables: Brush vegetables with olive oil and set on grilling sheet. Preheat grill to medium heat, and grill vegetables turning occasionally until cooked, about 7 to 10 minutes. Season with pepper. To serve, spread dill mayo inside pita and fill with grilled vegetables.

Serves 8

For the mayo: In a small bowl combine mayonnaise, yogurt, onion and dill. Cover and chill until ready to serve.

Nutrient Analysis per serving:	
Calories: 127	Fibre: 4 g
Carbohydrates: 18 g	Cholesterol: 3 mg
Total fat: 5 g	Protein: 4 g
Potassium: 413 mg	Sodium: 121 mg
Saturated Fat: 1 g	

MEAT & POULTRY

asian-style pork loins, p.57

creole beef skewers, p.65

DROP THAT 5LB STEAK!

Meat and poultry provide a great source of protein, iron, zinc and vitamin B12 but can also be high in saturated fat and cholesterol. Choosing leaner cuts and watching your portion size is key. Often the protein portion of the meal is considered the main focus but more emphasis should be put on vegetables. An ideal plate should consist of half vegetables, a quarter grain product and the last quarter protein. Most people are getting too much protein in their diet and are amazed that the actual recommended serving of 2 ½ - 3 oz is no larger than a deck of cards. Red meat can be high in saturated fat so limit your intake and eat more poultry, fish and seafood, and vegetarian dishes.

In this chapter you'll find a variety of mouth-watering meat dishes, such as the sweet but spicy Molasses Peppered Steak, the Asian-Style Pork with a hint of orange and sesame or the Creole Beef Skewers, a tasty alternative to the typical barbecue flavoured grilled meat skewers. If you're looking for a delicious way to dress up your poultry dishes, try the Peaches 'n' Chicken dish with a combination of barbecue sauce, peaches and water chestnuts.

peaches 'n' chicken, p.59

thai soy peanut molasses chicken

John's Prime Rib Steakhouse, Saskatoon, SK

This delicious sauce tastes great with chicken but you can also enjoy it with beef or fish. Although not necessary, marinate the chicken overnight in the refrigerator to get the full flavour. I cut back on the sesame oil but it still has a hint of sesame flavour.

1 tbsp (15 mL) garlic, minced
1 tbsp (15 mL) sesame oil
½ tbsp (7 mL) ground ginger
1 tbsp (15 mL) chili flakes
½ cup (125 mL) rice wine vinegar
1 tbsp (15 mL) sodium-reduced soy sauce
1 tbsp (15 mL) sugar
2 tbsp (30 mL) light peanut butter
1 tbsp (15 mL) molasses (preferably reduced-sugar)
½ cup (125 mL) water
4 boneless and skinless chicken breasts (3 oz / 85g each)

In a non-stick pan, sauté garlic in sesame oil over medium-low heat. Add ginger, chili, vinegar, soy sauce and sugar. Simmer for 5 minutes. Add peanut butter and molasses in stages. Bring to a boil, reduce to a simmer and gradually add water until desired consistency.

Preheat oven to 425°F (220°C). Pat chicken dry and coat chicken with half of the Thai sauce; place on a non-stick baking sheet. Bake for 12 to 15 minutes until no longer pink inside and juices run clear. Use reserved sauce to spoon over cooked chicken.

Serves 4

Nutrient Analysis per serving:

Calories: 209	Fibre: 1 g
Carbohydrates: 10 g	Cholesterol: 49 mg
Total fat: 9 g	Protein: 22 g
Potassium: 375 mg	Sodium: 194 mg
Saturated Fat: 2 g	

molasses peppered steak

The Willow on Wascana, Regina, SK

This dressing is a delicious complement to any meat or fish. Red meat tends to be higher in fat, especially unhealthy saturated fat, so be sure to trim off all fat. I have also cut back on the oil in this recipe.

4 sirloin steaks (3 oz / 85 g each), excess fat removed
1 clove garlic, minced
1 small shallot, minced
¼ cup (60 mL) molasses (preferably reduced-sugar)
½ tsp (2 mL) prepared mustard
1 ½ tsp (15 mL) ground pepper
1 ½ tsp (7 mL) canola oil
1 tbsp (15 mL) dark rum

Combine garlic, shallot, molasses, mustard and pepper. Slowly mix in oil and rum. Brush meat with half of dressing. Cook in non-stick frying pan over medium heat until cooked to preferred degree. Use the remainder of dressing to drizzle over cooked meat.

Serves 4

Nutrient Analysis per serving:	
Calories: 239	Fibre: 0 g
Carbohydrates: 18 g	Cholesterol: 48 mg
Total fat: 10 g	Protein: 18 g
Potassium: 648 mg	Sodium: 68 mg
Saturated Fat: 2 g	

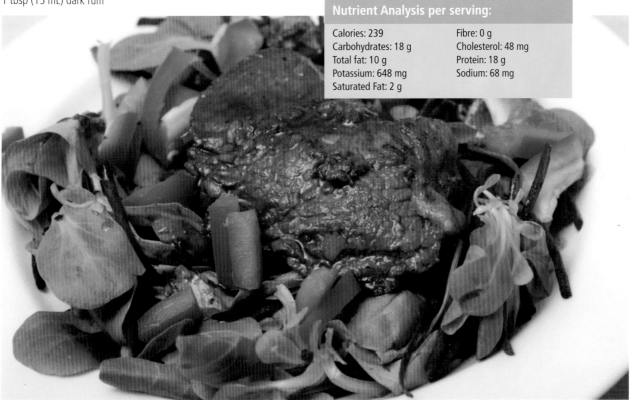

topless turkey apple burgers

Since hamburger buns tend to be high in sodium, I recommend eating only half of the bun; use a leaf of lettuce in place of the top bun. Animal products are a source of unhealthy saturated fat so it's important to choose extra-lean meats and trim off any excess fat. Avoid processed meats because they are very high in sodium. The recommended method to cook the burgers is on the grill but you can also cook them in a skillet on the stove. Serve them with a side salad of your choice.

1 ¼ lb (625 g) extra-lean ground turkey
½ cup (125 mL) whole wheat bread crumbs or unsalted soda crackers, crushed
½ cup (125 mL) finely diced onion
1 medium apple, cored, peeled and diced
½ tsp (2 mL) ground pepper
4 whole wheat hamburger buns
assorted condiments:
lettuce
tomato slices
red or green pepper strips
onion
relish, ketchup, mustard (limited amounts)

In a large bowl, mix together turkey, bread crumbs, onion, apple, and pepper. Shape meat into 8 patties, about the size of a deck of cards.

Preheat grill to medium-high. Cook burgers until no longer pink inside, turning as needed, about 8 to 10 minutes. The internal temperature of the burger must be 160°F (70°C). Serve immediately on a toasted bun with condiments of your choice, topped with a leaf of lettuce.

Serves 8

Nutrient Analysis per serving:	
Calories: 201	Fibre: 3 g
Carbohydrates: 18 g	Cholesterol: 56 mg
Total fat: 7 g	Protein: 16 g
Potassium: 379 mg	Sodium: 186 mg
Saturated Fat: 2 g	

asian-style pork loins

Susur Restaurant, Toronto, ON

To speed up the preparation time, I omitted marinating the meat and also put the sauce in the food processor so the vegetables do not need to be cooked separately. Despite these changes, the dish still turned out to be tasty and flavourful. This is excellent served over rice and your favourite vegetables. Be sure to look for sodium-reduced soy sauce; regular soy sauce is usually extremely high in salt/sodium.

6 boneless pork loins chops (3 oz / 85 g each)
1 medium stalk celery, coarsely chopped
1 medium carrot, coarsely chopped
1 medium onion, coarsely chopped
½ tbsp (7 mL) minced fresh ginger
zest and juice from ½ orange
⅓ cup (75 mL) dry sherry
1 tbsp (15 mL) sodium-reduced soy sauce
2 tbsp (30 mL) pure maple syrup
½ tbsp (7 mL) sesame oil

Preheat oven to 400°F (200°C). Trim loins of any excess fat, rinse and pat dry, and place in a lightly greased baking dish. In a blender or food processor combine celery, carrot and onion until finely chopped. Add ginger, orange zest and juice, sherry, soy sauce and maple syrup to vegetables; blend until combined. Slowly add sesame oil while blender is on low speed. Evenly cover pork with blended vegetable mixture. Cook for 10 to 15 minutes or until cooked. Reserve vegetable mixture from baking dish and serve over pork.

Serves 6

Nutrient Analysis per serving:

Calories: 177	Fibre: 1 g
Carbohydrates: 9 g	Cholesterol: 46 mg
Total fat: 7 g	Protein: 19 g
Potassium: 470 mg	Sodium: 216 mg
Saturated Fat: 2 g	

teriyaki steak and scallop stir-fry

The Whitman Inn, Caledonia, NS

I actually changed this recipe quite a bit — from a teriyaki appetizer wrap to a main course stir-fry — but kept the same sauce. Bottled teriyaki sauces are high in sodium and additives but this one is significantly healthier, equally delicious and easy to prepare. Although I prefer fresh vegetables over frozen, chopping can be quite time-consuming, so if time is an issue you can substitute frozen vegetables; I recommend using an oriental or Thai mixture. Place the vegetables in the microwave on defrost for several minutes to speed up the preparation time, and be sure to drain once defrosted.

1 ½ tbsp (22 mL) brown sugar
1 ½ tbsp (22 mL) honey
1 ½ tbsp (22 mL) sodium-reduced soy sauce
⅓ cup (75 mL) water
⅓ cup (75 mL) dry sherry
1 ½-inch piece fresh ginger, peeled and grated
3-4 cloves garlic, crushed
3 green onions, finely chopped
1 ½ tbsp (22 mL) cornstarch
2 tsp (10 mL) olive oil
½ lb (227 g) sirloin steak, cut into strips (remove fat)
½ lb (227 g) scallops
9 cups (2 L) mixed vegetables, in bite-size pieces
1 can water chestnuts
2 cups (500 mL) cooked long-grain instant brown rice

Make sauce by whisking together sugar, honey, soy sauce, water, sherry, ginger, garlic, green onion and cornstarch and set aside. Heat 1 tsp olive oil in a large non-stick skillet over medium heat. Add steak to skillet and sauté until cooked to preferred degree; remove from skillet. Heat the second teaspoon of oil in skillet and sauté mixed vegetables for approximately 4 to 5 minutes. Add sauce and continue to cook for 1 minute. Add steak, scallops and water chestnuts and sauté until scallops are opaque. Do not overcook. Serve stir-fry over rice.

Serves 6

Nutrient Analysis per serving:	
Calories: 420	Fibre: 14 g
Carbohydrates: 65 g	Cholesterol: 35 mg
Total fat: 5 g	Protein: 25 g
Potassium: 898 mg	Sodium: 269 mg
Saturated Fat: 1 g	

peaches 'n' chicken

The Palliser, Truro, NS

This is a delicious and simple chicken dish. If you are unable to find fresh peaches use canned peaches packed in juice. There is no need to cook for the additional 10 minutes if time is an issue. Just return the dish to the oven to bring it to serving temperature. Like most condiments, barbecue sauce is high in sodium; check the nutritional labels for the product with the lowest sodium. Serve this chicken with Orange-flavoured Rice with Cranberries and Cashews (p. 71) and salad.

2 tbsp (30 mL) flour
½ tsp (2 mL) paprika
6 skinless chicken breasts (3 oz / 85 g each), cut into 3 or 4 pieces each
¼ cup (60 mL) peach jam
¼ cup (60 mL) water
1 ½ tbsp (22 mL) barbecue sauce
3 tbsp (45 mL) diced onion
¼ cup (60 mL) diced green pepper
½ tbsp (7 mL) sodium-reduced soy sauce
¼ cup (60 mL) water chestnuts
¾ cup (175 mL) sliced peaches

Combine flour and paprika. Dredge chicken in flour mixture and lay pieces in a large shallow casserole dish. Preheat oven to 350°F (180°C). In a medium bowl, combine jam, water, barbecue sauce, onion, green pepper and soy sauce; pour over chicken pieces. Bake, uncovered, for 20 minutes or until cooked through and juices are clear. Add peach slices and water chestnuts and bake for an additional 10 minutes.

Serves 6

Nutrient Analysis per serving:

Calories: 164	Fibre: 1 g
Carbohydrates: 18 g	Cholesterol: 49 mg
Total fat: 1 g	Protein: 20 g
Potassium: 333 mg	Sodium: 168 mg
Saturated Fat: 0 g	

chicken breast exotic

Inn-on-the-Lake, Fall River, NS

This is a delicious and unique recipe. I have substituted fat-free yogurt for regular yogurt and the taste is still superb. Serve this chicken with your favourite vegetables and rice.

4 boneless and skinless chicken breasts (3 oz / 85 g each)
½ apple, diced
1 plum, diced
1 kiwi, diced
1 medium banana, diced
8 pieces pineapple, diced
1 ½ tbsp (22 mL) mango chutney
1 tbsp (15 mL) vegetable oil for browning

Curry sauce
½ cup (125 mL) plain fat-free yogurt
¼ tsp (1 mL) curry
dash of pepper

For the chicken: Prepare chicken by slicing a pocket in the side of each breast, being careful not to cut all the way through. Toss fruit and chutney together in a bowl. Set aside half of fruit mixture; divide rest of fruit mixture into 4 portions and stuff into pockets in chicken breasts. Preheat oven to 350°F (180°C). Add oil to skillet and cook chicken for 3 minutes on each side until browned. Transfer to a non-stick baking sheet and bake until cooked, approximately 15 to 20 minutes.

Spoon curry sauce over cooked chicken, followed by reserved fruit mixture.

Serves 4

For the curry sauce: Combine yogurt, curry and pepper.

Nutrient Analysis per serving:

Calories: 226	Fibre: 2 g
Carbohydrates: 24 g	Cholesterol: 49 mg
Total fat: 5 g	Protein: 22 g
Potassium: 535 mg	Sodium: 82 mg
Saturated Fat: 1 g	

chicken lemonato

Opa Greek Taverna, Halifax, NS

Lemon adds a nice fresh citrus taste to this Greek dish. The original recipe also calls for shrimp but it is high in cholesterol and the recipe is equally tasty with chicken.

¾ lb (340 g) boneless chicken breasts, sliced into strips
flour for dredging
1 tbsp (15 mL) olive oil
10 thin slices of lemon
1 large red pepper, in julienne strips
¾ cup (175 mL) white wine
1 tbsp (15 mL) freshly chopped parsley for garnish

Dredge chicken strips in flour, shaking off excess. Heat oil in a non-stick skillet over medium heat and brown chicken strips. Add lemon and red pepper and sauté for 2 minutes. Add wine and sauté until chicken is cooked and juices are slightly reduced. To serve, place strips of chicken on plate, top with red peppers and lemon slices and garnish with parsley.

Serves 4

Nutrient Analysis per serving:

Calories: 159
Carbohydrates: 6 g
Total fat: 5 g
Potassium: 333 mg
Saturated Fat: 1 g

Fibre: 1 g
Cholesterol: 49 mg
Protein: 20 g
Sodium: 58 mg

red wine cranberry rhubarb chutney over turkey

Buffalo Mountain Lodge, Banff, AB

Similar to cranberry sauce, this chutney combines rhubarb, cinnamon and citrus. It tastes great with turkey or chicken. The longer you cook it, the thicker it gets. I prefer it when there is still some liquid remaining as opposed to a thicker cranberry sauce-like version.

Red wine cranberry rhubarb chutney

¼ cup (60 mL) sugar
2 ½ tbsp (35 mL) freshly squeezed orange juice
¼ tsp (1 mL) orange zest
¼ cup (60 mL) red wine
½ cup (125 mL) cranberries
⅔ cup (150 mL) rhubarb
2-inch (10-cm) cinnamon stick
1 tsp (5 mL) pepper
grated fresh ginger

Turkey

¾ lb (340 g) turkey breast, cut into 4 pieces
flour for dredging
1 tbsp (15 mL) vegetable oil

For the chutney: Combine all chutney ingredients in a covered saucepan over medium-high heat. Once mixture starts to boil, remove cover. Cook until cranberries burst and mixture thickens.

Makes 1 cup (250 mL)

For the turkey: While chutney is cooking, prepare turkey. Dredge turkey breast in flour. Heat oil on a non-stick skillet over medium-high heat, add turkey and sauté until cooked through. Top turkey with chutney and serve.

Serves 4

Nutrient Analysis per serving:	
Calories: 241	Fibre: 1g
Carbohydrates: 17 g	Cholesterol: 55 mg
Total fat: 9 g	Protein: 19 g
Potassium: 347 mg	Sodium: 51 mg
Saturated Fat: 2 g	

pork with curried pineapple chutney

The Dundee Arms Hotel, Charlottetown, PEI

This fruit chutney is great with pork. The original recipe recommends simmering the chutney for one hour but this is not required. I did cut back on the liquid so it is not too watery.

2 tsp (10 mL) vegetable oil, divided
½ medium red onion, chopped
½ medium red pepper, chopped
1 ½ tbsp (22 mL) jalapeño pepper, seeded and minced
2 tsp (10 mL) curry powder
2 cups (500 mL) fresh pineapple cubes (or pineapple canned in juice, drained)
¼ cup (60 mL) orange juice
¼ cup (60 mL) cider vinegar
2 tbsp (30 mL) brown sugar
6 boneless pork chops (3 oz / 85 g each)

Heat 1 teaspoon (5 mL) of oil in a heavy saucepan over medium-high heat. Add red onion and red pepper and sauté, stirring frequently, until onion begins to soften. Add jalapeño and curry powder, stirring for 1 minute. Add pineapple, orange juice, cider vinegar and brown sugar and cook chutney, stirring frequently, for several minutes then cover and let simmer on low. In the meantime, in a separate non-stick skillet, heat the remaining teaspoon of oil on medium heat, add pork and cook until done. Serve pork topped with chutney or for a complete meal and great presentation, serve this dish with brown rice and chutney topped with pork. Store any leftover chutney in the refrigerator.

Serves 6

Nutrient Analysis per serving:

Calories: 194	Fibre: 1 g
Carbohydrates: 13 g	Cholesterol: 46 mg
Total fat: 7 g	Protein: 19 g
Potassium: 481 mg	Sodium: 41 mg
Saturated Fat: 2 g	

maple apple pork

Inn on the Cove, Saint John, NB

Pork and apples make a great combination. The original recipe uses a full pork tenderloin but I recommend the boneless loin steaks or cutting tenderloin into medallions prior to cooking to cut down on the cooking time. I also omitted the liqueur and still found it was full of flavour.

6 portions boneless pork loin steaks (3 oz / 85 g each)
2 tsp (10 mL) canola oil
paprika
3 apples, peeled and sliced
½ medium onion, chopped
2 tbsp (30 mL) maple syrup
¼ cup (60 mL) reduced-sodium chicken stock
½ tsp (2 mL) thyme
pepper to taste

Heat oil in a non-stick skillet over medium heat; add pork and sprinkle with paprika. Cook until browned and remove from pan. Add apples, onion and maple syrup to pan and sauté until lightly browned. Add chicken stock and bring to boil. Return tenderloin to pan; add thyme and spoon mixture over tenderloin. Cook until meat is tender and only slightly pink. Remove meat from pan and serve topped with apple and onion mixture. Add pepper to taste.

Serves 6

Nutrient Analysis per serving:

Calories: 201	Fibre: 1 g
Carbohydrates: 16 g	Cholesterol: 46 mg
Total fat: 7 g	Protein: 19 g
Potassium: 462 mg	Sodium: 62 mg
Saturated Fat: 2 g	

creole beef skewers

Cathedral Freehouse, Regina, SK

Mustard is very high in sodium, especially Dijon mustard. The original recipe called for a large amount of Dijon but I substituted prepared yellow mustard and cut back on the amount to make it more heart-healthy. Serve these beef skewers over salad and with a whole wheat pita or serve in a wrap with vegetables.

1 ½ tbsp (22 mL) yellow mustard
3 tbsp (45 mL) water
3 tbsp (45 mL) molasses (preferably reduced-sugar variety)
2 tbsp (30 mL) light mayonnaise
2 tbsp (30 mL) fat-free plain yogurt
1 tbsp (15 mL) white wine vinegar
1 tsp (5 mL) Worcestershire sauce
¼ cup (60 mL) minced onion
¼ cup (60 mL) diced tomato
pinch of turmeric and pepper
½ tsp (2 mL) fresh thyme
½ tbsp (7 mL) minced fresh garlic
1 lb (500 g) beef sirloin, excess fat removed, cut into
   1-in (2.5-cm) cubes

Mix all ingredients except beef in a small bowl to make a creamy sauce. Divide sauce evenly into 2 bowls. Toss and coat beef with one portion of sauce then thread beef onto skewers. Grill over medium heat until beef is cooked to preferred degree. Use reserved sauce to drizzle over meat.

Serves 6

Nutrient Analysis per serving:

Calories: 174	Fibre: 0 g
Carbohydrates: 10 g	Cholesterol: 52 mg
Total fat: 7 g	Protein: 18 g
Potassium: 467 mg	Sodium: 138 mg
Saturated Fat: 2 g	

VEGGIES & SIDES

orange-flavoured rice with cranberries and cashews, p.71   glazed asparagus and tomatoes, p.75

HOLD THE SALT AND GO FOR VEGGIES!

Vegetables and side dishes do not have to be plain and boring. These recipes are easy and healthy ways to add extra flavour to your meal without high fat and salt. Vegetables always taste their best when they are in season and fresh. When possible, purchase your produce from fruit and vegetable stands and farmers markets to support local farmers and the environment and to obtain guaranteed freshness.

To bring flair to plain steamed rice, add some fruit and nuts to make Orange-flavoured Rice with Cranberries and Cashews. For a tomato-based rice try Sun-dried Tomato Rice Pilaf. Couscous is becoming more and more popular but many people are unsure how to prepare it. For a tasty couscous with a little zip, try Spicy Tomato and Spinach Couscous. As for vegetable sides, Zucchini with Pine Nuts is guaranteed to be a hit.

herb and garlic roasted mini potatoes, p.73

zucchini with pine nuts

This is a healthy and delicious way to dress up zucchini. The pine nuts add a great crunch and flavour.

1 tsp (5 mL) vegetable oil
3 medium zucchinis, cut into ¼-in (5-mm) slices
½ oz (15 g) pine nuts

Heat oil in a medium-sized skillet over medium heat. Add zucchini and sauté until slightly tender, about 3 minutes. Add pine nuts and continue to sauté about 1 minute. Serve warm.

Serves 4

Nutrient Analysis per serving:

Calories: 57	Fibre: 2 g
Carbohydrates: 5 g	Cholesterol: 0 mg
Total fat: 4 g	Protein: 2 g
Potassium: 406 mg	Sodium: 15 mg
Saturated Fat: 0 g	

spicy tomato and spinach couscous

Couscous is one of my favorite grains and very easy to prepare. It can be used in place of rice and pasta at most meals. Whole wheat couscous is preferable due to the higher fibre content but if you are unable to find it, regular will work as well.

1 cup (250 mL) whole wheat couscous
1 tbsp (15 mL) olive oil
1 clove garlic, minced
¼ cup (60 mL) diced onion
½ cup (125 mL) diced yellow pepper
½ tsp (2 mL) cumin
1–2 tsp (5–10 mL) cayenne
1 tbsp (15 mL) chili powder
3 tbsp (45 mL) tomato paste
1 cup (250 mL) no-added-salt diced tomatoes, drained
3 cups (750 mL) fresh spinach

Place couscous in a medium-sized bowl and prepare as per package directions with boiling water. Use fork to fluff. In the meantime, heat oil in a large non-stick skillet over medium heat. Add garlic, onion and yellow pepper and sauté for 2 minutes. Add cumin, cayenne and chili powder and sauté for 1 minute. Stir in tomato paste, tomatoes and spinach and cook until heated through and spinach is wilted, approximately 4 minutes. Add couscous and combine well.

Serves 6–8

Nutrient Analysis per serving:

Calories: 131	Fibre: 3 g
Carbohydrates: 21 g	Cholesterol: 0 mg
Total fat: 4 g	Protein: 4 g
Potassium: 270 mg	Sodium: 22 mg
Saturated Fat: 1 g	

orange-flavoured rice with cranberries and cashews

This makes a great side dish, especially with a sweet/fruity-flavoured meat or poultry dish.

2 cups (500 mL) cooked instant brown rice
juice of 1 orange
¼ cup (60 mL) cashew pieces
⅓ cup (75 mL) dried cranberries
2 green onions, chopped
2 tbsp (30 mL) minced cilantro

Add juice to rice and mix well. Add cashews, cranberries, onion and cilantro and combine.

Serves 4–6

Nutrient Analysis per serving:	
Calories: 202	Fibre: 3 g
Carbohydrates: 37 g	Cholesterol: 0 mg
Total fat: 5 g	Protein: 4 g
Potassium: 206 mg	Sodium: 4 mg
Saturated Fat: 1 g	

sun-dried tomato rice pilaf

Val D'Isère Restaurant, Whistler, BC

The original recipe was a sun-dried tomato risotto but like all risotto it calls for Arborio rice, a longer-cooking rice. I really love the flavour so I tried it with instant brown rice — it turned out fine and preparation time was cut back. Enjoy this rice as a side or topped with meat or fish.

1 cup (250 mL) instant brown rice
1 cup (250 mL) low-sodium chicken broth or vegetable broth
1 tbsp (15 mL) olive oil
2 tbsp (30 mL) minced garlic
¼ cup (60 mL) minced shallots
3 tbsp (45 mL) no-added-salt tomato paste
3 tbsp (45 mL) dry-packed sun-dried tomatoes, chopped
3 tbsp (45 mL) diced tomatoes
3 tbsp (45 mL) grated Parmesan cheese
pepper to taste

Prepare rice as per package directions but replace water with chicken broth. Heat oil in a large non-stick skillet over medium heat; add garlic and shallots and sauté for 1 minute. Add prepared rice and tomato paste; combine. Mix in tomatoes, sun-dried tomatoes and Parmesan cheese; season with pepper to taste.

Serves 4–6

Nutrient Analysis per serving:

Calories: 171	Fibre: 2 g
Carbohydrates: 29 g	Cholesterol: 0 mg
Total fat: 4 g	Protein: 5 g
Potassium: 292 mg	Sodium: 99 mg
Saturated Fat: 1 g	

herb and garlic roasted mini potatoes

Potatoes sometimes get a bad rep for being unhealthy and fattening but the truth is they are quite nutritious, providing a source of potassium, fibre and vitamin C. There are several different varieties of mini potatoes, including red, yellow and purple. Choose a mixture or whichever variety you prefer but keep in mind the darker in color, the higher the nutrient value.

1 lb (500g) mini potatoes
1 tbsp (15 mL) olive oil
2 tbsp (30 mL) chopped fresh parsley
1 tsp (5 mL) chili powder
1 tsp (5 mL) garlic powder
pinch chili flakes (optional)

Clean potatoes; cut larger ones in quarters and smaller ones in half. Place in bowl, toss with oil and season with remainder of ingredients. Transfer potatoes to a baking sheet. Bake at 425°F (220°C) for 20 minutes or until tender.

Serves 4

Nutrient Analysis per serving:	
Calories: 115	Fibre: 2 g
Carbohydrates: 20 g	Cholesterol: 0 mg
Total fat: 4 g	Protein: 2 g
Potassium: 509 mg	Sodium: 8 mg
Saturated Fat: 1 g	

summer garden vegetables

Elaine Elliot and Virginia Lee

You can use any combination of vegetables in season; just make sure the cooking times are similar. These vegetables can be prepared on the grill or in a wok/skillet on the stove.

2 tsp (10 mL) vegetable oil
2 cloves garlic, minced
½ medium red onion, wedged
6 cups (1.5 L) summer vegetables cut into bite-sized pieces:
  broccoli, green beans, wax beans, asparagus, celery, baby carrots,
  bell peppers, zucchini, sugar snap peas, snow peas, shelled peas,
  cherry tomatoes, corn kernels
2 tbsp (30 mL) fresh lemon juice
1 tsp (5 mL) lemon zest
pepper to taste

In a large heavy-based skillet or wok, heat oil over medium-high heat. Add garlic and onion and cook, stirring constantly, about 1 minute. Add slow-cooking vegetables such as carrots, asparagus, zucchini, green and wax beans; cook, stirring constantly, for 2 minutes. Adjust heat as necessary throughout cooking process to prevent burning. Add quick-cooking vegetables such as bell peppers, celery, peas and tomatoes; cook, stirring constantly, for 2 minutes.

During the last minute of cooking you may need to cover and steam the vegetables to be sure they are cooked crisp-tender. Remove cover and splash with lemon juice. Sprinkle with lemon zest and season with pepper.

Serves 6

Nutrient Analysis per serving:	
Calories: 55	Fibre: 3 g
Carbohydrates: 9 g	Cholesterol: 0 mg
Total fat: 2 g	Protein: 2 g
Potassium: 326 mg	Sodium: 21 mg
Saturated Fat: 0 g	

glazed asparagus and tomatoes

This is a simple, high-potassium side dish that can accompany any main course.

1 tsp (5 mL) vegetable oil
1 clove garlic, minced
1 ½ lb (750 g) asparagus, trimmed and cut into 1-in (2.5-cm) pieces
1 ½ cups (375 mL) cherry tomatoes
1 tbsp (15 mL) minced fresh ginger
2 tbsp (30 mL) balsamic vinegar
1 tbsp (15 mL) honey

Heat oil and garlic in a medium non-stick skillet over medium-high heat until fragrant. Add asparagus and sauté for about 3 minutes. Add cherry tomatoes, ginger, balsamic vinegar and honey; sauté until tomatoes start to soften and burst open.

Serves 4

Nutrient Analysis per serving:	
Calories: 74	Fibre: 4 g
Carbohydrates: 14 g	Cholesterol: 0 mg
Total fat: 1 g	Protein: 4 g
Potassium: 482 mg	Sodium: 7 mg
Saturated Fat: 0 g	

DESSERTS

citus fruit salad with pistachios and honey, p.84

warm rainforest crunch bananas, p.79

HOLD THE SALT — AND ENJOY DESSERT!

Who would ever imagine you can have your cake and eat it too? Dessert is my favourite part of the meal and for all those with a similar sweet tooth: you're bound to find something here to satisfy your craving. Unlike most traditional 'empty calories' desserts, I have chosen a selection of healthier lower fat, lower calorie and higher nutrient desserts. Calories can be cut back in most recipes by making simple substitutions such as using cocoa in place of chocolate, or yogurt and apple sauce in place of oil or butter, by using reduced-fat cream and milk in place of regular cream or milk and by cutting out a quarter of the sugar. Keep in mind though, moderation still has to be considered.

Choose a dessert for any occasion! The Scandinavian Apple Cake or Pumpkin Spice Cupcakes with Cinnamon are a healthier choice than the traditional birthday cake. If you are looking for a unique dessert, wow your guests with Warm Rainforest Crunch Bananas. For lighter fare, try Citrus Fruit Salad with Pistachios and Honey or Maple Sabayon on Marinated Berries.

mini chocolate brownie bites, p.86

pumpkin spice cupcakes with cinnamon frozen yogurt

Thyme and Again Creative Catering, Ottawa, ON

The original recipe is a pumpkin spice cake but to decrease the cooking time, I changed it to cupcakes. The original called for a high-fat maple glaze but I replaced it with a cinnamon frozen yogurt topping for a lighter choice that's still a nice way to dress it up. I also cut back on the oil by substituting yogurt, decreased the sugar and replaced some of the all-purpose flour with whole-wheat flour. If you have high cholesterol, you may want to substitute egg whites for the whole eggs.

Cupcakes

⅓ cup (75 mL) vegetable oil
3 tbsp (45 mL) fat-free plain yogurt
1 cup (250 mL) granulated sugar
2 eggs (or 4 egg whites)
1 cup (250 mL) all-purpose flour
¾ cup (175 mL) whole wheat flour
2 tsp (10 mL) cinnamon
½ tsp (2 mL) nutmeg
½ tsp (2 mL) allspice
½ tsp (2 mL) baking powder
½ tsp (2 mL) baking soda
1 cup (250 mL) pumpkin purée
½ cup (125 mL) skim milk

Cinnamon vanilla yogurt topping

2 cups (500 mL) frozen vanilla yogurt
cinnamon

For the cupcakes: Preheat oven to 350°F (180°C). Line 18 muffin cups with paper baking liners.

In a large bowl, mix together oil, yogurt and sugar with a hand mixer until light and fluffy. Add eggs one at a time, making sure each one is well incorporated before adding the next egg. In a separate bowl, sift dry ingredients together and in another bowl mix together pumpkin purée and milk.

With the hand mixer on low speed, add ⅓ of the dry ingredients to the sugar/oil mixture, followed by ⅓ of the milk/purée mixture, mixing well after each addition. Continue to alternately add wet and dry ingredients until mixtures are all combined.

Divide batter among muffin cups and bake for 25 to 35 minutes or until a cake tester comes out clean. Remove from oven and cool on wire rack.

Serve warm or at room temperature, with a dollop of frozen vanilla yogurt, topped with a sprinkle of cinnamon.

Makes 1 ½ dozen

Nutrient Analysis per serving:

Calories: 177	Fibre: 1 g
Carbohydrates: 28 g	Cholesterol: 24 mg
Total fat: 6 g	Protein: 4 g
Potassium: 167 mg	Sodium: 90 mg
Saturated Fat: 1 g	

warm rainforest crunch bananas

Herald Street Caffe, Victoria, BC

This dessert is delicious and one of my favourites. Bananas are tasty to begin with but even better combined with nuts, coconut and phyllo.

2 tbsp (30 mL) toasted pecan pieces*
2 tbsp (30 mL) toasted coconut*
2 large ripe bananas, peeled
2 sheets phyllo pastry
2 tbsp (30 mL) non-hydrogenated soft margarine, melted
icing sugar
cocoa

Combine nuts and coconut and spread out on a flat surface. Roll bananas in nut mixture, pressing firmly to coat well. Set aside. Place 1 sheet of phyllo on work surface and brush with 1 tablespoon of margarine. Lay 1 banana at one end of phyllo; roll up, folding in sides. Repeat with remaining banana, phyllo and margarine.

Lightly brush banana roll-ups with melted margarine. Bake in 350°F (180°C) oven for 10 minutes or until pastry is golden brown. To serve, cut each roll-up in half and dust lightly with icing sugar and cocoa. Serve warm.

Serves 4

*A quick way to toast pecans and coconut is in a skillet on medium heat, tossing frequently, for several minutes until golden and fragrant.

Nutrient Analysis per serving:	
Calories: 184	Fibre: 2 g
Carbohydrates: 24 g	Cholesterol: 0 mg
Total fat: 10 g	Protein: 2 g
Potassium: 285 mg	Sodium: 98 mg
Saturated Fat: 0 g	

strawberry and apricot empress scones

Fairmont Hotel, Victoria, BC

At the Fairmont these scones are intended as a snack with tea, with strawberry preserves and cream, but I find them sweet enough to be enjoyed as dessert. I wanted to incorporate more strawberries and apricots to increase the potassium and nutrient content. If fresh or canned apricots are difficult to find, use dried ones (soft, or re-hydrated by soaking in warm water for 20 to 30 minutes). I also substituted whole wheat flour for some of the all-purpose flour and skim milk for the cream, and they still turn out moist and fluffy. I did cut back on the baking powder to decrease the sodium (salt) content but it is still higher than desired, so limit your intake to one scone and watch your sodium intake throughout the day, or only have half a scone with lots of fruit. They also taste great topped with a small scoop of frozen yogurt.

Scones

2 cups (500 mL) all-purpose flour
1 cup (250 mL) whole wheat flour
½ cup (125 mL) sugar
1 ½ tbsp (30 mL) baking powder
⅓ cup (75 mL) non-hydrogenated soft margarine
2 eggs + 1 egg white
1 cup (250 mL) skim milk
⅓ cup (75 mL) raisins (optional)
1 tbsp (15 mL) water

Topping

2 ½ cups (625 mL) frozen strawberries, thawed, with juices
2 ½ cups (625 mL) sliced apricots (fresh or canned)
3 tbsp (45 mL) sugar

For the scones: In bowl, sift together flours, sugar and baking powder. Add margarine and blend with fingertips until mixture is mealy. (Be careful not to over-work.) Lightly beat 2 eggs with milk and blend into mixture until just combined. Mix in raisins until just combined.

Spoon batter (about 2 tablespoons at a time) onto a lightly greased baking sheet. Whisk together egg white and water and brush over scones.

Bake in 325°F (160°C) oven for 16 to 18 minutes, until scones are golden brown.

For the topping: Combine defrosted strawberries, apricots and sugar. Warm in microwave for several minutes. Cut scones in halves and serve topped with warm fruit.

Makes 1 ½ dozen

Nutrient Analysis per serving:

Calories: 118	Fibre: 2 g
Carbohydrates: 21 g	Cholesterol: 18 mg
Total fat: 3 g	Protein: 3 g
Potassium: 135 mg	Sodium: 236 mg
Saturated Fat: 1 g	

classic apple crisp with vanilla yogurt

Mountain Gap Inn and Resort, Smith's Cove, NS

Apple crisp is always a crowd-pleaser and an easy dessert to prepare.

6 apples, peeled, cored and sliced
2 tbsp (30 mL) lemon juice
¼ cup (60 mL) sugar
½ cup (125 mL) whole wheat flour
3 tbsp (45 mL) brown sugar
2 ½ tbsp (45 mL) non-hydrogenated soft margarine
½ tsp (2 mL) cinnamon
vanilla fat-free yogurt

Preheat oven to 350°F (180°C). Toss prepared apples with lemon juice and sugar and spread out in a 9 x 9-in (22 x 22-cm) pan. In a bowl, combine margarine, brown sugar and cinnamon until crumbly. Sprinkle evenly over apples and bake until apples are tender and the top is golden brown, about 30 to 35 minutes. Serve warm with a dollop of yogurt.

Serves 8

Nutrient Analysis per serving:

Calories: 167	Fibre: 2 g
Carbohydrates: 33 g	Cholesterol: 1 mg
Total fat: 4 g	Protein: 3 g
Potassium: 201 mg	Sodium: 50 mg
Saturated Fat: 1g	

scandinavian apple cake

Seven Restaurant & Wine Bar, Halifax, NS

The apples make this cake moist and delicious. It's a perfect way to use the apples in your fridge.

⅓ cup (75 mL) vegetable oil
½ cup (125 mL) sugar
1 egg
1 tsp (5 mL) vanilla
1 tsp (5 mL) baking powder
1 tsp (5 mL) baking soda
1 tsp (5 mL) ground cinnamon
1 tsp (5 mL) allspice
½ tsp (2 mL) cardamom
1 cup (250 mL) all-purpose flour
2–3 apples, peeled, cored and chopped

Preheat oven to 350°F (180°C). Lightly grease a 9 x 9-in (22 x 22-cm) baking dish.

In a large bowl, beat oil and sugar until light in colour. Mix in egg and add vanilla. Sift in dry ingredients, mix until blended, then fold in the apples. Pour into prepared baking dish and bake for 20 to 25 minutes until cake tester comes out clean. Cool on a wire rack for 15 minutes.

Serves 12

Nutrient Analysis per serving:	
Calories: 150	Fibre: 1 g
Carbohydrates: 22 g	Cholesterol: 18 mg
Total fat: 7 g	Protein: 2 g
Potassium: 54 mg	Sodium: 148 mg
Saturated Fat: 1 g	

citrus fruit salad with pistachios and honey

This is a nice light dessert that won't leave you feeling overly full. Pink grapefruit is a great addition to this salad but if you are on prescription medication, check with your pharmacist first because it can cause interactions. You can also choose from a variety of oranges, such as Cara Cara oranges, Mineola oranges, etc.

2 large navel oranges, peeled, sectioned and chopped into bite-sized pieces
2 tangerines, peeled, sectioned and chopped into bite-sized pieces
3 clementine oranges, peeled and sectioned
1-2 mandarin oranges (or 1 can mandarin oranges drained)
¼ cup (60 mL) raw unsalted pistachio nuts, shelled and chopped
1 tbsp (15 mL) honey

Mix all fruit and nuts in a bowl. Divide fruit and nut mixture among 4 small serving bowls; drizzle with honey and serve.

Serves 4

Nutrient Analysis per serving:

Calories: 152	Fibre: 4 g
Carbohydrates: 30 g	Cholesterol: 0 mg
Total fat: 4 g	Protein: 3 g
Potassium: 402 mg	Sodium: 4 mg
Saturated Fat: 0 g	

mini chocolate brownie bites

These are any chocolate lover's dream. You'll be surprised these are low-fat because they are packed with satisfying chocolate flavour.

½ cup (125 mL) all-purpose flour
½ cup (125 mL) whole wheat flour
½ cup (125 mL) cocoa
1 tsp (5 mL) baking powder
2 tbsp (30 mL) vegetable oil
1 ¼ cups (310 mL) sugar
1 egg
½ cup (125 mL) fat-free plain yogurt or unsweetened apple sauce
2 tsp (10 mL) vanilla

Preheat oven to 350°F (180°C). Lightly grease 24 mini muffin cups.

Sift flours, cocoa, and baking powder into a mixing bowl. In medium bowl combine oil, sugar, egg, yogurt/apple sauce and vanilla. Add flour mixture to wet mixture and mix until just combined.

Fill muffin cups ¾ full with batter. Bake for 18 to 20 minutes or until cake tester comes out clean.

Makes 2 dozen

Nutrient Analysis per serving:

Calories: 154	Fibre: 2 g
Carbohydrates: 31 g	Cholesterol: 0 mg
Total fat: 3 g	Protein: 3 g
Potassium: 112 mg	Sodium: 53 mg
Saturated Fat: 0 g	

'grand-pères' au sirop d'érable with blueberries

Parker's Lodge, Val-David, QC

These are maple-flavoured dumplings that are so simple to prepare and so delicious. You can top them up with dessert topping, vanilla yogurt or vanilla frozen yogurt. I also added fresh blueberries to the recipe but you can use whichever berry you prefer.

¾ cup (175 mL) maple syrup
1 ¼ cup (310 mL) water
1 cup (250 mL) all-purpose flour
2 tsp (10 mL) baking powder
1 tbsp (15 mL) non-hydrogenated soft margarine
½ cup (125 mL) skim or 1% milk
1 cup (250 mL) fresh blueberries
vanilla frozen yogurt

In a deep pot, combine maple syrup and water and bring to a boil. In a bowl, whisk together flour and baking powder. Cut in margarine with a pastry blender and stir in milk to make a soft dough. Drop the batter by spoonfuls on top of the simmering maple sauce. Immediately cover saucepan and cook over medium heat without removing cover for 12 to 15 minutes. Serve warm with sauce; top with a small scoop of vanilla frozen yogurt and blueberries.

Serves 8

Nutrient Analysis per serving:

Calories: 194	Fibre: 1 g
Carbohydrates: 40 g	Cholesterol: 1 mg
Total fat: 3 g	Protein: 4 g
Potassium: 155 mg	Sodium: 157 mg
Saturated Fat: 1 g	

molasses oatmeal cookies

Kamloops Catering, Rocky Mountaineer Railway, Kamloops, BC

Usually molasses-based cookies are not my favourite but these are a definite exception. They are great served with a cup of tea or a glass of milk. I was able to decrease the amount of sugar and fat and they still taste wonderful. I also used old-fashioned rolled oats instead of quick-cooking oats and didn't find a significant difference. If you prefer a crispier cookie, allow them to bake for a few additional minutes.

¾ cup (175 mL) sugar
⅓ cup (75 mL) vegetable oil
1 egg
⅓ cup (75 mL) molasses
1 cup (250 mL) all-purpose flour, sifted
1 cup (250 mL) whole wheat flour
1 ½ tsp (7 mL) baking soda
1 tsp (5 mL) vanilla extract
1 cup (250 mL) old-fashioned rolled oats
1 cup (250 mL) raisins
½ cup (125 mL) chopped walnuts

Mix together sugar and oil in a large mixing bowl, add egg and molasses and beat well. Add flour and baking soda and mix well. Add vanilla and stir in oats, raisins and nuts. Drop batter from a teaspoon onto a lightly greased baking sheet. Bake at 375°F (180°C) for 8 to 10 minutes.

Makes about 48 to 55 cookies

Nutrient Analysis per serving (2 cookies):

Calories: 132	Fibre: 1 g
Carbohydrates: 21 g	Cholesterol: 0 mg
Total fat: 5 g	Protein: 3 g
Potassium: 102 mg	Sodium: 77 mg
Saturated Fat: 0 g	

maple sabayon on marinated berries

Harvest Dining Room, Fairmont Hotel MacDonald, Edmonton, AB

This is a simple and light dessert packed with lots of vitamins, minerals and antioxidants from the berries. If you have high cholesterol, cut back on the amount of egg and sugar mixture you put over the berries.

4 cups (1 L) seasonal berries (strawberries, raspberries, blueberries, etc.)
¼ cup (60 mL) Grand Marnier liqueur
1 egg + 1 egg white
2 tbsp (30 mL) granulated sugar
2 tbsp (30 mL) maple syrup
3 tbsp (45 mL) white wine
mint leaves, for garnish

Place berries in a bowl and drizzle with Grand Marnier. Spoon into 4 heatproof bowls and set aside.

Continually whisk egg, egg white and sugar in a heatproof bowl until foamy and pale. Set bowl over pan of simmering water. Whisk constantly, adding maple syrup and wine a little at a time, until mixture is fluffy and thickened.

Preheat broiler. Spoon sauce over berries and brown under broiler until golden, 2 to 3 minutes. Serve immediately, garnished with mint leaves.

Serves 4

Nutrient Analysis per serving:

Calories: 145	Fibre: 6 g
Carbohydrates: 29 g	Cholesterol: 53 mg
Total fat: 2 g	Protein: 4 g
Potassium: 250 mg	Sodium: 34 mg
Saturated Fat: 0 g	

THE FACTS

DAILY NUTRIENT GOALS

(USED IN THE DASH STUDIES FOR A 2100 CALORIE EATING PLAN)

Total fat	27% of calories
Saturated fat	6% of calories
Protein	18% of calories
Carbohydrates	55% of calories
Cholesterol	150 mg
Sodium	1500 to 2300 mg*
Potassium	4700 mg
Calcium	1250 mg
Fibre	30 g

*Researchers recommend that most people should consume less than 2300 mg of sodium a day.
Middle-aged and older individuals who already have high blood pressure should limit sodium to
no more than 1500 mg.

POTASSIUM IN YOUR DIET

Sodium is the mineral that gets the most attention when it comes to blood pressure. Another mineral that deserves more attention for its effect on blood pressure is potassium. Potassium is found in many fruits and vegetables, meat, whole grains and legumes. Research shows that a diet rich in potassium plays a significant role in lowering blood pressure. The US Food and Drug Administration supports a potassium-rich diet as being an effective way to lower high blood pressure and the risk for stroke. Although potassium supplements are available, they are not proven to be as effective as potassium obtained from food. The DASH diet recommends 4700 mg of potassium a day. This is an easy step you can take for your health without making a significant sacrifice. The majority of the recipes in this cookbook are high in potassium.

WHAT IS ONE DASH SERVING?

Grains and grain products	1 slice of bread, preferably whole grain
	½ pita bread or ½ tortilla
	½ medium-sized bagel
	½ cup (125 mL) cooked cereal, pasta or rice
	1 oz (30 g) cold cereal, such as bran flakes
	2 graham crackers or 4 soda crackers
Vegetables	1 cup (250 mL) raw leafy vegetables
	½ cup (125 mL) cooked vegetables
	½ cup (125 mL) vegetable juice
Fruits	1 medium fruit
	½ cup (125 mL) fresh, frozen or canned fruit
	½ cup (125 mL) fruit juice
	¼ cup (60 mL) dried fruit
Low-fat dairy products	1 cup (250 mL) milk
	1 cup (250 mL) yogurt
	1 ½ oz (45 g) cheese
Meat, poultry and fish	1 oz (30 g) portion
Nuts, seeds and legumes	⅓ cup (75 mL) or 1 ½ oz (45 g) nuts
	2 tbsp (30 mL) or 1 ½ oz (45 g) seeds
	½ cup (125 mL) cooked dried beans / legumes
	2 tbsp (30 mL) peanut butter
	3 oz (85 g) tofu
Fats and oils	1 tsp (5 mL) soft margarine or vegetable oil
	1 tsp (5 mL) regular mayonnaise
	1 tbsp (15 mL) low-fat regular mayonnaise
	1 tbsp (15 mL) regular salad dressing
	2 tbsp (30 mL) light salad dressing
Sweets	1 tbsp (15 mL) maple syrup
	1 tbsp (15 mL) sugar
	1 tbsp (15 mL) jam or jelly
	½ cup (125 mL) sherbet
	½ cup (125 mL) low-fat or non-fat frozen yogurt

SHAKE THE SALT OUT OF YOUR DIET!

11 STEPS TO HELP GET YOU THERE:

1. Be cautious with certain headache and heartburn medications which may contain sodium bicarbonate or carbonate.

2. Do not add salt while cooking or at the table.

3. Cooking from scratch is the best method to control what is going into your food.

4. Avoid or limit seasonings and sauces that are high in sodium, such as soy sauce, chili sauce, steak spice / sauce, salsa, meat tenderizer, bouillon, barbecue sauce, mustard and ketchup.

5. The sodium content in similar products can vary significantly. Always compare labels and portion sizes, especially with cereals, cheeses, canned and frozen products, breads and crackers.

6. Season your food with lemon, garlic, pepper, herbs, etc. Be cautious with prepared seasonings — always check the ingredients.

7. Avoid adding salt to your cooking water for pastas, rice, vegetables, etc.

8. Choose fresh or frozen meat, poultry and fish rather than processed and canned products.

9. When dining out ask the server for lower-sodium options and / or ask that your meal be prepared without salt.

10. Salt substitutes are available but you should always consult with your physician prior to using them, in case of kidney problems.

11. Check out the sodium content in many common foods, especially from fast food restaurants.

DASH PUBLICATIONS

"DASH eating plan." US Department of Health and Human Resources. Retrieved from: www.nhlbi.nih.gov/health/public/heart/hdp/dash/new_dash.html, April 20, 2009.

"The DASH diet to lower high blood pressure." The Heart and Stroke Foundation. Retrieved from www.heartandstroke.ns.ca/site/c.inKMIPNlEiG/b.4122193/k.9DC7/The_DASH_Diet_to_lower_blood_pressure.htm

Mahan, K. & Escott-Stump, S. (2004). *Krause's Food, Nutrition, & Diet Therapy* (11th Edition). Philidelphia, PA: Elsevier.

Nolan, Sandra (2008). *Delicious DASH Flavours*. Halifax, NS: Formac Publishing Company Limited.

Sizer, F. & Whitney, E. (2003). *Nutrition: Concepts and Controversies* (9th ed.). Belmont, CA: Wadsworth.

Whitney, E.N., Cataldo, C.B. & Rolfes, S.R. (2002). *Understanding Normal and Clinical Nutrition* (6th ed.). Belmont, CA: Wadsworth.

CREDITS AND THANKS

PHOTOGRAPHY

All interior photos by Alanna Jankov, except where noted below:

Carole Gomez: 21, 23; Dirk Richter: 63, 73; iStock: 15, 31, 33, 49, 72, 74; James McQuillan: 25, 47; Janet Kimber: 88; Jean Gill: 69, 75; Karen Wiesner: 17; Meghan Collins: 50; Robert Dant: 87; Ronda Tyree: 13, 42; Stuart Brown: 55

FOOD STYLING

Special thanks to Michael Howell, Chef / Proprietor at Tempest World Cuisine in Wolfville, Nova Scotia, and Executive Chef at The Port Gastropub in Port Williams, Nova Scotia, for preparing and styling the recipes photographed for this book.

HAIR AND MAKEUP

Hair by Orla MacEachern
Thumpers Salon

Make-up by Jennifer Stewart
Breathe Esthetics & Massage Therapy

INDEX